W9-BBK-447

WITHDRAWN

WITHDRAWN

The Language Arts
in Elementary Schools

THE LIBRARY OF EDUCATION

A Project of The Center for Applied Research in Education, Inc.

G. R. Gottschalk, Director

Advisory Board:

Ralph W. Tyler, Chairman
C. Ray Carpenter
Harold C. Case
Theodore A. Distler
Henry H. Hill
Monsignor Frederick G. Hochwalt
Paul A. Miller
Edgar L. Morphet
Harold G. Shane
Harold Spears

Editorial Board:

Walter A. Anderson, Chairman
John S. Brubacher
Eric F. Gardner
Daniel E. Griffiths
John Dale Russell

Categories of Coverage

I	II	III
Curriculum and Teaching	Administration, Organization, and Finance	Psychology

IV	V	VI
History, Philosophy, and Social Foundations	Professional Skills	Educational Institutions

The Language Arts
in Elementary Schools

WALTER T. PETTY

Associate Professor of Education
Sacramento State College

CARL A. RUDISILL LIBRARY
LENOIR RHYNE COLLEGE

1962
The Center for Applied Research in Education, Inc.
Washington, D.C.

370
L61

© 1962 BY THE CENTER FOR APPLIED
RESEARCH IN EDUCATION, INC.
WASHINGTON, D.C.

ALL RIGHTS RESERVED. NO PART OF THIS BOOK
MAY BE REPRODUCED IN ANY FORM, BY MIMEO-
GRAPH OR ANY OTHER MEANS, WITHOUT PER-
MISSION IN WRITING FROM THE PUBLISHERS.

LIBRARY OF CONGRESS
CATALOG CARD NO.: 62–18290

44 581
February, 1963

PRINTED IN THE UNITED STATES OF AMERICA
52274

Foreword

In the following discussion, of which this is a brief introduction, Dr. Walter T. Petty presents a timely and concise summary of many persistently important issues confronting the practicing teacher and the pupil-learner in the development of mastery of the essentials of language expression in the first six grades of the elementary school. The manner of treatment is not that of a language text, a teacher's manual, or a methods book. It is written in language the teacher understands on issues of recognized significance to the teacher of language expression. Much of the merit of the treatment stems not only from the author's own extensive experience in the classroom as teacher and supervisor, but also from his disposition to dig deeply and select carefully from the rather rich sources of research available in this field.

It is a timely discussion because teachers in the English language classroom are constantly in need of assistance in crystallizing and in putting into practice the best that is known in point of view, purposes of instruction, methods of motivating and perfecting learning, as well as the essentials of materials and methods of instruction and evaluation. It is concise in that, while it is based upon the results of research wherever possible, it interprets the research in the form of concrete procedures for the teacher to use rather than by citing the research itself.

While the treatment at the outset is correctly directed to the problems of creating in the classroom the atmosphere essential to the stimulation of correct language expression, it is equally concerned with the consideration of practical methods by which the most effective principles of motivation, learning, and evaluation may be applied in the formation of socially acceptable language habits. The discussion, while pointed directly at the classroom teacher, avoids the assumption that the point of view of the modern program of developing expressional skills, or the other issues dependent thereon are necessarily understood and accepted by the reader. Accordingly, numerous excellent suggestions are given on the general philosophy of language as it affects the content of the language curriculum at each of the major instructional levels and in each of the major skill areas. Equally helpful hints for motivating learning, habituating skills, and evaluating results are also presented in proper order.

In addition to providing these above-mentioned practical aids to the classroom teacher, this discussion presents (for the supervisor and other practical educators close to the classroom as well as for students and others interested in elementary education) a brief account of the program and procedures in one of the most vital of the social skill areas—that of developing effective and acceptable habits of language expression on the part of the oncoming generations.

HARRY A. GREENE
Emeritus Professor of Education
State University of Iowa

Contents

The Language Arts
in Elementary Schools

CHAPTER I

The Language Curriculum

Often the critic of American education—including the "man on the street"—considers himself an authority on what should be included in a school curriculum. As most teachers and many other persons who have active interest in public education are well aware, however, the critic's ideas on curriculum content are apt to be hazy in his own mind—and are certainly unclear to educators. Everyone tends to be an expert on schools until he is asked to cite evidence supporting his views. This fact is regrettable but it shows the need for teachers to determine more firmly what is to be taught and to establish more clearly the reasons for this determination.

A Philosophical Basis

The attitudes toward education held by teachers and non-teachers alike at various times in our history have markedly influenced the school curriculums of their day, as well as that which has evolved into today's curriculum. As we have progressed as a people, we have increasingly learned more about the nature of man and how he learns, the nature of language, and the role of school and teacher in man's development. Today, the curriculum in language—or the language *arts*—is based upon this knowledge.

The nature and function of language. Language is a tool—perhaps man's most basic tool. It would be difficult for men to live together, think, or act without the sounds and symbols of language. It is almost impossible to imagine life without language—a life without conversation, writing, books, mass communication media, and thoughts based upon language-developed concepts. There is little doubt, too, that as the complexity of our civilization increases the importance of language as a tool increases. As scientific achievement shrinks the world, men are giving greater and greater attention to the development of universal communication in order to maintain civilization. In the same way that the family group must communicate in order to live a human life, so must all men communicate to preserve an increasingly complex world.

Using language is not an innate human ability—it must be learned. Although animals have the physical capacity to produce sounds, and in some instances they may even have learned that particular reactions occur when they make these sounds, only man has the physical and mental endowments necessary to develop true language. Language is more than instinctive sounds given in response to environmental conditions; it is a system for interpreting and organizing experience, as well as for communicating ideas and feelings. Language and the thoughts and feelings derived from experience are highly interrelated.

Man's use of language is the result of long trial, imitation, and practice. He early found the need for making responses to situations, especially those involving feeling and emotion. At first this was done by gestures, facial expressions, and cries. Once the situation stimulating the response, the primitive communicative act itself, and the subsequent response from other human beings which this act stimulated became common to all members of a group, definite meaning began to be attached to these gestures, facial expressions, and cries—they had become natural signs with meaning.

As the use of natural signs became common, the next logical step was taken when man recognized that sounds—and later, written symbols—could be attached not only to the communicative act itself (or a portion of it) but also to the reaction it caused in other men. With the development of these symbols, man began to use them in his thinking processes. Thinking itself is actually the manipulation of various symbols which have meanings attached to them. Thus, before systemizing language symbols as we know them, man made use of other symbols in his thinking; but the process of living with others—particularly as society became more and more complex—brought a greater need for the development of language symbols and for their use in man's thinking.

While language is used for communication and for thinking, a third function derives from the other two. As man communicated, thought, developed new ideas, and found the need for passing on to succeeding generations more than the very simplest things, language has been his means for transmitting culture from generation to generation. Without language men would be isolated from one another, would not be able to share thoughts and ideas, and would know little of other people, places, and times.

While language is used in performing the functions of communication, thinking, and recording, it is not the same for each individual. Even within an identical cultural setting each individual's language is uniquely his. Since a word is a symbol, it has no meaning or even sound of its own. It is true, that agreements as to sound and meaning have been made among men, but these are general in nature. For each individual there is a personal meaning to each language symbol that he knows; no one else knows exactly what this meaning is. Each person using a language symbol has had a personal experience with that symbol. This fact in the nature of language cannot be ignored, since communication is language's chief function and since communication is dependent upon common understanding of the symbols used. The implications of common experience in helping language function are clear.

The purposes of language instruction. Teachers in the past considered language to be a static, unchanging subject—something taught and used only in English class. There was a "correct" language, one that was always the same, and one that when learned was suitable for all times and places. Teachers gave no thought to change but concentrated upon maintaining the "purity" they felt was there, the tradition that must be upheld. Perhaps if this were true the task of instruction in the use of language would be relatively simple. But it is not true, and most educators today are aware of the vital nature of language, and of how it changes. More and more it is recognized that an acceptable usage in one situation is not necessarily suitable in another; that words and meanings have been added and that others have been lost or have changed; and that language is functional and fluid, with its principal purpose being to promote communication. Language is now recognized as something alive, changing, and, along with culture, evolving. Thus, language must be functional for communication actually to occur.

The major purpose of the school, as it has been for centuries, is to help prepare children to meet adequately the problems of life, and to find their places in the expanding culture. How this may best be done, and what it means in terms of instruction, has always been a matter for debate. Various approaches have been made but in recent years increasing attention has been given to analyses of society to determine the knowledge, habits, attitudes, and skills important and likely to be needed by the child—both as a child and as an adult—in that society. Thus, the language taught is that which is used: the words most frequently employed in writing, the punctuation most needed, the usages which make effective communication possible, and handwriting that is legible.

Learning Language

Children come to school with considerable knowledge in using language. They have heard a language spoken for five or six years; they have spoken it themselves for nearly that long. Their achievement has largely been accomplished by imitating those with whom they have been in contact. They have heard the sounds made by others and have themselves gradually formed words; they have observed the effects of these words when spoken and have thus become aware of meaning. Their adjustment to a language world has been gradual and has varied from child to child, but each one has learned to say the words he has heard and has attached meaning as it was attached by those around him.

All of this suggests that a child surveys his environment, appraises it, and directs his action in terms of it. He explores and learns; in fact, the normal process of learning is by exploration. It suggests further that a child is directed and limited in his exploration or learning by his environment. Thus, the factors influencing the language growth of a child are the rate of his maturation and the world that constitutes his knowledge. Limitations in maturity and in experience limit language growth. Too, language development itself is a vital part of the total growth process, a part of adjusting to life, of giving meaning to experiences, of bringing order to a bewildering environment. Again, language and experience are closely interrelated.

As one describes a child's pre-school language education, so should one characterize his school education. When a classroom offers a variety of rich human activity, with full opportunity for participation, language will be learned. Language becomes an inextricable function of this activity and these experiences. The school must foster natural conditions for learning, for exploration. It must be an ideal environment, rich in things, activities, people, and ideas. The remarkable language achievements of children before they enter school is unmistakable evidence for the structuring of the school's program along these lines. This evidence reveals the true purpose of the school's program and the only sound way to achieve the purposes sought. The goal must be to foster exploration and to expand and improve learning, not to limit it or to block communication by suppressing natural activity and arresting inherent drives to learn.

Organizing for Language Instruction

The school program in language, as with any subject area, should operate on the principle of accepting each child as he is, with the obligation of providing instruction to take care of his individual needs. At the same time, however, concern must be shown for promoting the greatest growth possible for all the children in a class. Thus, the selection of and emphasis on language knowledge and skills for a particular class is determined both by the needs of individual pupils and by the common needs of all. Further, a good language program does not leave to chance the determination and development of the abilities needed, but it provides for their introduction and instruction in a systematic fashion. Such a program provides for the teaching of language both in connection with everyday classroom activities and during specific periods set aside for that purpose.

The primary task in the organization of a class program is the setting of goals—defining as clearly and as accurately as possible just what should be accomplished. This may be done in a series of steps, the first being an examination of the school's curriculum guide or course of study, followed by the making of a tentative listing of class goals. Second, from a similar scrutiny of the textbooks to be used for the grade level, the tentative listing is refined. The results of these steps indicate the "normal" expectancy for the class, but should not be regarded as a final determination of appropriate goals for a particular class.

The third step is the crucial one of deciding which goals are appropriate for the specific group. Usually this step must be of a subjective nature. It should, however, be based upon a reasonably systematic evaluation through the use of checklists and similar informal appraisal instruments, testing how well the children tell stories, make reports, write compositions, spell, punctuate, and so forth. This third step should also involve the use of more formal standardized and teacher-devised tests of important abilities and skills. At this point, the activities and the skills, abilities, and attitudes to be stressed in the program must be rather precisely determined and stated. The remaining step is one of deciding each child's needs in relation to these goals. Again, this is best done through a series of informal tests and introductory lessons on each phase of the proposed program—tests and lessons which may be analyzed and the results recorded for reference as the program is further planned, developed, and modified.

The instructional unit. Learning experiences in language should be organized around lifelike situations and activities—situations and activities which constantly provide opportunities for experiences closely related to the children's personal and social needs. The instructional emphasis should be upon participation in the practical use of language rather than upon training for its use. The situations and activities selected should be those that give opportunity for the functional use of the skills and abilities demanded in real-life language situations. Children are best motivated for language learning when they can sense the practical need of a particular skill; they are motivated as they are convinced that the skills and abilities being taught serve genuine and lifelike purposes. Children are slow to accept artificiality but are not slow in recognizing it.

Instructional units may be built upon the naturally occurring events of the classroom—those of a social nature and those that deal with subject matter. No contrived motivation is necessary; children are already interested in these situations. No contrived content for speaking, listening, reading, and writing need be supplied; the content is already present. In social studies, for example, as children study the history and geography of America, there are many occasions for writing letters, giving reports, outlining information, building vocabulary, and using indexes in locating information. There is also much to talk and write about, to listen to, and to read. In science, again there is occasion for writing summaries, records, and reports as well as for discussion and conversation. Daily in the classroom, in the give and take of being together, children may also learn to listen to one another, to speak with clarity and accuracy, to write for communicative purposes, and to read so that they may more effectively participate. In the classroom they also will have need for language courtesy, making introductions and accepting and extending greetings to one another or to parents and other visitors. In these situations and in many others the use of language is natural and practical, and is so recognized by the children themselves.

In considering an instructional unit in language for a particular grade level—and for a particular class—major attention must be given to the utilization of the lifelike events and naturally occurring activities emphasized above. In the actual planning phase of a unit, however, many practical questions arise. Questions as to the unit's relation to other units, the specific skills to emphasize, the general abilities to stress, the amounts of instruction to give on the various skills or abilities, and the performance levels to strive for are all critical and must be answered. Answers to these questions are not all readily forthcoming from the events and activities themselves. It is conceivable that events and situations might occur in a classroom so that language use naturally takes place, and yet no genuine language learning results. A teacher planning an instructional unit must take into account things other than the situations. He must know the principles of learning; he must have an understanding of the total curriculum goals, and those specifically applicable to achievement in language instruction; and he must have knowledge of the language skills, abilities, and understandings important in the lives of children and adults, as well as the ones which are most crucial, which are most frequently used, and which are most difficult to learn. With due attention to these things, and utilizing the situations presented, instructional units can be developed.

Caring for individual differences. Within a total language program for a school, for a particular class within that school, or for a specific unit of instruction, careful attention must be given to the wide deviation of language skill development among children. Even a flexible program as suggested here—a program based upon reasonable goals indicated by textbooks and curriculum guides, and modified in terms of class and individual needs—requires further adaptation in terms of instructional procedures.

Grouping. This procedure calls for the division of a class into smaller groups according to abilities or interests, or learning purpose. For example, a teacher's survey of class needs may show that thirteen of his thirty-two pupils rather consistently make errors in the use of commas to set off appositives, another twelve pupils may show difficulty mastering the form of the business letter, and the remaining seven pupils, having no difficulty with these two items, may be interested in preparing written summaries of activities they have carried on in connection with the science unit. Thus, there is clear-cut reason for dividing into smaller units for instruction. Such grouping, however, should be informal, flexible, and of a duration long enough only to accomplish the specific tasks. Sometimes any one group may receive direct instruction from the teacher; at other times a group may work alone and the children explore and learn together. Grouping has definite limitations that are readily apparent. The principal one is that any child's ability, needs, and interests tend to differ from any other's. Thus, the grouping procedure still places a child in an instructional situation which only partially provides for him as an individual. Too, a child who is deficient or retarded in one aspect of language use, or in one language situation, tends to be deficient or retarded in others, and there is often little actual flexibility operating.

Individualizing assignments. This procedure is an extension of the grouping idea but attempts to satisfy the limitations of grouping by assignment of tasks to an individual pupil rather than to a group. As an example, all members of a class might be preparing reports for a social studies unit but the reports might be of differing degrees of difficulty. One child might be seeking information for a report on the foods the pioneers ate; another might be writing the conversation two wagon masters might have had before leaving with their wagon trains; a third might be preparing a critique of a western television show; and a fourth might be tracing routes on a map. The task of each child depends upon his interest and his ability. The child searching for names of foods may have limited reading and writing skills, so he is essentially engaged in finding words and listing them. The child writing conversation must have read extensively, and must be fairly skilled in writing. Each child's task should challenge him, however, and in order to be of value in teaching language skills, should call for the use of some of these skills— particularly those he needs most. In addition, the use of this procedure does not mean that a teacher can absent himself from the group. On the contrary, the teacher must actively aid the learning of each individual child.

Laboratory approach. This procedure is essentially one of individual attention to needs and is most suitable for instruction in written expression. As children write, each one writing something that has purpose for him, the teacher moves from child to child giving help, suggestions, and encouragement. The assignments do not necessarily need to be individualized, since the children may all be writing stories about Halloween, or may all be writing summaries of a chapter in a textbook. What each child writes, however, is individualized. No set pattern is established; no minimum or maximum length is required; and the teacher actively works with each child.

Team learning. This procedure is another modification of the basic concept of grouping in that each child in the class is paired or grouped with another. In some instances the two children of a team may be of comparable ability in what they are doing; in others, one child may have greater knowledge and/or skill. Children need not have equal handwriting or spelling ability to help and to test each other. They may need to be more nearly of equal ability in order to prepare reports or to practice punctuating sentences.

Programmed instruction. Again, this procedure is not basically different from other attempts to individualize instruction, but it is more carefully planned in its presentation of materials to be learned than is usually the case in the procedures described previously. Essentially, programmed instruction works by providing facts and questions in amounts that the learner can assimilate and master before moving on to others. Sometimes these small amounts of material are presented mechanically, such as by showing one frame of a film at a time; at other times the materials to be taught are presented in a more-or-less standard textbook fashion. The principal features distinguishing a programmed textbook or a programmed "visual" for teaching-machine presentation from regular textbooks and film materials are that the learner must finish one step (answer the question, etc.) before moving on to the next, and that the materials are designed for individual rather than group use. Programmed instruction has met with some success in the teaching of spelling and obviously could be used to teach punctuation and capitalization skills, as well as others of the more mechanical language skills.[1]

Special activities. Additional approaches and activities which focus upon individual development include:

1. Having each pupil keep lists of words misspelled, usage errors frequently made, capitalization errors, ideas for writing, and so on.

2. Having pupils do extra work such as making charts of abbreviations, synonyms, or action words; preparing bulletin boards; and doing creative writing.

3. Allowing pupils to choose their own topics for oral reports and for writing activities.

4. Providing individual correction of usage errors and doing individualized practicing upon correct usage habits that need to be established.

---

[1] Douglas Porter, "Some Effects of Year-Long Teaching Machine Instruction," in *Automatic Teaching: The State of the Art,* ed. Eugene Galanter (New York: John Wiley & Sons, Inc., 1959), pp. 85–90.

CHAPTER II

The Foundational Period
of Language Instruction

Language development is a continuous process that begins at birth and continues throughout life. The period a child spends in the primary grades is usually regarded as one of transition from the informal language learning done primarily in the home to that of the more formal instruction which takes place in school. In spite of the transitional nature of the early grades, however, many of the same activities are stressed in learning language expression at any grade level. The primary goals of expression are the basis for early instruction in school, but there is no major demarcation in the program for most children between grades two or three and the remainder of the elementary school grades. Therefore, much that is said in later chapters concerning the teaching of oral and written language skills and abilities applies equally to the primary grades.

The Role of Early Home Training

A child truly begins to learn language when he first hears someone speak. He learns early that his first instinctive cries mean something to his mother and that certain sounds she makes call for responses from him. Thus, communication begins almost with birth. A baby's natural impulse is to vocalize and to imitate those around him, his attempts gradually leading to intelligible and meaningful sounds. He is then well on the way to using language in his thinking and communicating.

For most children starting school the knowledge of words and their use is quite extensive. The average child at this stage is able to use at least 2500 different words in his speech and able to understand perhaps ten times that number.[1] Any generalizations, how-

---

[1] See Dorothea McCarthy, "Language Development in Children," in Leonard Carmichael, ed., *Manual of Child Psychology* (New York: John Wiley & Sons, Inc., rev. ed., 1954), for a summary of studies of language development in children.

ever, about the "average" may mean little to the kindergarten or first-grade teacher since the thirty or so boys and girls will have come from such varied backgrounds and be in such varied stages of language development that there is probably no common starting point. The children will be alike in that the language habits they have will be rather firmly established. They will not question the "correctness" with which they speak; they will not have thought about whether their habits are "good" or "bad"; they will remember that when they have spoken they have usually been understood. Language will not have been regarded by them as a problem.

With their arrival at school the language situation may change rapidly. A child may be ill at ease in the new social situation. He may have done little talking with other children, or he may have used baby talk or a private language with his family. Suddenly he discovers that these new persons do not understand him. On the other hand, he may have frequently been told to keep quiet, or he may have had his speaking ignored. Now he finds that he is expected to talk and that others are listening to him. It is not unusual for a child not to understand the teacher or other children completely; new vocabulary is often presented rapidly. All of these language difficulties encountered by children just entering school indicate the need for a transition from home to school and the importance of having language readiness programs which precede actual language instruction.

Language Readiness

A readiness program in language is much more than just a period of inactive waiting for maturation. It consists of planned activities leading up to the more formal instruction encountered later. Although the language development of each child is limited by his maturity and cannot successfully be hastened, each level of development may be sharpened in preparation for greater maturity. The language readiness program takes advantage of the language development which children bring to school and builds upon this development in preparation for the later acquisition of effective oral and manual expression skills.

Most primary teachers think of over-all language-arts readiness programs rather than readiness programs in individual areas such as reading or speaking. They recognize the role that language development plays in readiness for all learning, that our schools are language schools, and that the use of language is interrelated with every function of the school. Nearly all that children learn in school is gained through experiences involving actual use of language. Therefore, a school's readiness program begins on the first day a child enters school and continues to function in providing readiness for each successive step in learning.

The beginning readiness program is initially concerned with the child's attitudes toward language and toward learning in general. This concern must also continue through later steps toward achieving truly effective expression. Children without the desire to learn will not learn; neither will they achieve a readiness to learn.

Basic too in developing language readiness as well as creating motivation is the provision for an adequate fund of experience with language. The room environment must be conducive to learning; there must be many things going on of interest to children—things they will think and talk about. Words must be made interesting and ways of speaking must appeal. Without these no real interest in language will develop.

Language readiness also involves habits of attentiveness. Effective listening and courtesy in communication depend upon attentiveness. Getting children to be attentive is largely the result of adequately varied activity in the classroom combined with proper control of the class by the teacher. Language is used in social situations; communication implies two or more people (a social setting) using language. For children to have adequate experiences with language the group must operate together. They must respect one another and one another's rights. The teacher who has social control of his or her class recognizes social settings for language and also that success in providing the needed fund of language experience depends upon this social control.

Language Objectives of the Primary Grades

The range in language abilities shown by children entering the primary grades presents a problem in the establishment of instructional objectives. Children are at varying levels of language development and show varying attitudes toward learning. In addition, an individual child may reveal surprising variations in ability, skill, and interest. He may have a relatively large vocabulary of understood words, yet show considerable immaturity in making certain sounds. He may be a skillful storyteller, yet be careless in language usage. Such differences must be recognized and dealt with. Helping children develop interest and basic skill in using language is the principal task of kindergarten, first- and second-grade teachers. A broad statement of objective is not enough, though, to plan genuinely for instruction. The need for an organized program of instruction, however, does require statements of desired outcomes as a logical first step in such planning. One source lists these general objectives:[2]

1. Spontaneity of expression.
2. Socialization.
3. Enunciation and voice control.
4. Correct usage.
5. Organization of thought.

The desire to express himself is instinctive in a child; but he may often feel unable or unwilling to do so. The primary goal, then, is to build in him a confidence that he has something to say by providing many opportunities for enriching experiences and for imparting to others his reactions toward those experiences. Spontaneity of expression comes both from having plenty to talk about and from the stimulation of an understanding teacher.

Each child comes to school very much an "individual." Often he may have had little experience in taking turns at talking or other related activities; he may not be interested in listening to others; or he may feel awkward with other children and with the teacher. It becomes a major task in the primary grades to teach children to share ideas and materials, to develop responsibility both as individuals and members of groups, and to acquire courteous and socially accepted habits of behavior in action and speech.

At every grade level the development of genuine effectiveness in oral expression depends to a large extent upon an easy and pleasant manner in speaking, good voice control in both volume and tone, and accurate articulation and clear enunciation when speaking. Attention must be given to needs in these areas as soon as children

---

[2] Harry A. Greene and Walter T. Petty, *Developing Language Skills in the Elementary School* (Boston: Allyn and Bacon, Inc., 1959), pp. 66–67.

enter school. Some speech difficulties may require the services of a speech specialist and some children may be lacking in maturity, but other errors and undesirable habits may be remedied through attention in the instructional program.

A mechanical aspect of language expression which requires the same constant attention in the kindergarten and primary grades as it does in later grades is the formation of habits of using acceptable words and phrases. The habits of usage that children have when entering school often need changing—a difficult task since five or six years have been spent in establishing them and the many hours of the day when the children are not in school help continue these habits. However, the sooner an attempt is made at correction, and the greater the persistence with which the attempt is pursued, the greater the likelihood of actually educing improvement.

A word of caution is necessary in regard to establishing acceptable usage: attempting to correct every error a child makes may develop self-consciousness and an unwillingness to talk. The teacher must exercise judgment as to the emotional makeup of individual children, and must put each objective into perspective with the others.

The last objective—organization of thought—should not be thought of as needing less attention than the others or of receiving attention after the other objectives have been attained. Children should begin learning to organize their thinking in their first kindergarten activities, and continuing attention must be given in the other primary grades to this extremely important aspect of effective expression.

While it is almost impossible to assign specific language skills for mastery at a particular grade level, it is desirable to focus the program upon even more specific objectives than those discussed in order for teachers not to emphasize the same things that the other teachers have emphasized. Analysis of class and individual needs would, of course, prevent needless re-emphasis. But often a teacher may need reminding of this—and statements of grade-to-grade objectives may provide such a reminder.

Oral language. A minimal list of objectives for the various grade levels should properly be developed by the teachers of these grades in a particular school. Such a list might include the following:

KINDERGARTEN

1. Enrichment of children's vocabularies through provision for many experiences.

2. Development of the ability to describe simple events briefly with reasonable accuracy and clarity, and without excessive self-consciousness.

3. Encouraging development of the ability to use complete sentences rather than unclear fragments.

4. Sparking interest in language and in the improvement of its use by attention to enunciation, pronunciation, and clear diction.

5. Fostering of interest in listening to poems and stories and to their retelling.

6. Development of the ability to participate in simple dramatizations.

FIRST GRADE

In addition to continuing emphasis on kindergarten goals, the program should focus on:

1. Further development of the ability to express ideas clearly and in short sentences.

2. Development of the ability to use and to distinguish between declarative and interrogative sentences.

3. The showing of politeness by correctly using *please, excuse me, thank you, good morning,* and *good night.*

4. The regular use of *yes, no,* and *what,* rather than *uh-huh, naw,* and *huh.*

5. Improving usage by the substitution of such expressions as *I haven't a* or *I have no* for *I haven't no.*

6. Developing the ability to listen attentively and courteously.

SECOND GRADE

The second grade should give attention to:

1. Further development in saying something with the sentences in proper sequence.

2. Articulating clearly such word endings as *d, t,* and *g.*

3. The elimination of monotony of tone in speaking.

4. The ability to tell the two or three most important ideas involved before relating a story.

5. The ability to use *and* correctly in a series.

6. The ability to tell stories accurately and interestingly.

7. The habitual use of *haven't any, have not, them, those, went,* and *gone* in correctly phrased expressions.

8. The ability to describe a book, giving the author, title, and some point of interest.

Written language. An adequate foundational oral language program will have made the children language conscious, will have established certain usage standards, and will have begun the establishment of attitudes and abilities favorable to learning the skills and habits necessary for effective written expression. There are specific written language objectives, however, that point to skills and habits which should be developed in the primary grades. Again, while these are best determined with specific children in mind, the following may be representative of such objectives:

KINDERGARTEN

1. Providing for individual and class dictated sentences, stories, and letters written by the teacher.
2. Regular teacher use of such terms as *sentence, capital letter,* and *period.*

FIRST GRADE

1. Continuation of the program of group dictation.
2. Development of the ability in each child to:
   a. Write his full name.
   b. Find the date on a calendar and copy it correctly.
   c. Copy several simple sentences from the board.
   d. Write two or three short sentences about one thing.
   e. Begin sentences with capital letters and end them with a period or question mark.

SECOND GRADE

1. Continued development of skill in using manuscript writing.
2. Development of the ability to:
   a. Write the names of the school, city, and state (or correctly abbreviate them).
   b. Correctly fill in simple completion exercises and information forms.
   c. Capitalize correctly the names of persons, days, months, holidays, cities, and so forth used in regular writing.
   d. Write a simple note or friendly letter correctly using *Miss, Mr.,* or *Mrs.*
3. Development of skill in arranging work, including using margins and writing in straight lines.

Language Instructional Emphasis

The informality of the school program in the primary grades provides the ideal setting for teaching language expression. As children converse about their activities, discuss projects, excursions, and interests; and relate their experiences, real and imagined, unlimited opportunities are presented for the accomplishment of the objectives cited above. The teacher in the primary grades must be concerned with the teaching of language in all activities. Such teaching does not consist, though, of always stopping a conversation or a discussion, or stopping a game on the playground, to correct errors in usage, articulation, or the child's thinking. The teacher, however, should always note errors made, generally by written note, so that correction can be worked upon at an opportune time. Much improvement in the children's use of language may also be accomplished through the use of situations in which the children as an audience react to the child who is speaking, through occasional incidental correction, and through the constant awareness of the teacher that his own language is a model which the children will imitate. In addition to the teaching that results from this careful utilization of the many informal language situations, more specific teaching procedures are necessary in other more systematic and organized situations.

Storytelling. Storytelling in the primary grades includes: (1) the reproduction of stories which the child has read or has had read or told to him; (2) stories "made up" by the child, perhaps based in part upon stories heard or read; and (3) accounts or stories of the child's personal experiences. All of these are discussed in the following chapter and in the section on creative writing. Aspects dealing with the primary grades are discussed here.

Primary teachers probably encourage the telling of personal experiences more than any other form of storytelling. While Jimmy may readily volunteer, "Yesterday, I went to the zoo with my uncle. We saw elephants, lions, and monkeys—an' fed them peanuts, too," a number of children in every classroom are much more reluctant to talk before the entire group. Many will talk little to the teacher and not at all to the class. These children need much encouragement and stimulation. The reluctance to speak may be because of either a lack of social experience or a deficiency in experiences which may be related, or of both. Teachers sometimes become discouraged in their attempts to teach even the more talkative children to describe personal experiences because of the lack of organization of the children's thinking and of the often uninteresting nature of many things they relate. Many difficulties presented in teaching children to discuss personal experiences may be avoided by:

1. Having them talk about an object—perhaps a picture or drawing—rather than an abstract subject.

2. Helping them discover experiences they have had that would interest the class. Things told do not have to be accounts of major happenings but can be rather minor things—something that is special to the child alone. The teacher must be particularly observant in order to do this.

3. Having a child tell of his experience to a small group within the class rather than to the entire class.

4. Doing some screening of stories ahead of the telling time. This will allow the teacher to make suggestions to the teller and also help prepare the class to be better listeners.

5. Having the relating of experiences, or the describing of an object, done at various times throughout the day rather than just during the "share and tell" periods.

To reproduce stories successfully requires that the children have heard or read many stories. Since children are only learning to read in the primary grades the burden of this intake is upon the teacher and his skill in the telling of stories. Stories that are effectively retold by children are those that have appealed to them. Thus the teacher must tell many stories, must tell a wide variety of stories, and must tell them well in order for all of the children to be stimulated into retelling.

These suggestions may prove helpful:

1. Have a storytelling hour; perhaps have several groups telling stories during this hour, each with a chairman and organized to take turns in telling.

2. Establish storytelling standards; do this cooperatively and keep the standards posted.

3. Discuss storytelling—how stories are told, what kinds of stories are liked best, what stories they have heard at home, and who can tell a good story and why.

4. Encourage the children to comment constructively about stories that are told to them.

Dramatization. Children in the primary grades do much play-acting if they are given the opportunity. Dramatic play, and the more formalized dramatization, are natural outgrowths of children's thinking about their interests and they will engage in it naturally in their play and communication activities, both at home and at school.

Dramatization in the primary grades should not always be done for an audience, although occasionally an audience of adults or of other children will aid the development of language skills and create pleasure for the actors. Any dramatization before an audience should retain some elements of informality; for example, lines do not need to be memorized verbatim. It is better for the children to know the selection so well that they have the "feel" of the characters.

Primary grade children may often be first interested in pantomime —pretending with concentration and without speaking. This activity may be used to help children get accustomed to performing before others, while the teacher or an extroverted pupil reads the speech and describes the action. Often, too, pantomime may lead to the children getting the "feel" of the story so that they apply words to their actions. Sometimes the pantomiming of a story may lead to the children suggesting that they should write a story themselves and act it out. All of the possibilities for dramatization should be utilized and made parts of a total program for achieving the language objectives.

Hearing and speaking poetry. The use of poetry to develop interest in language, to teach proper listening, to build vocabulary and concepts, to stimulate expression, and to enjoy its rewards should be a part of every language program. It is particularly true that young children love to hear poetry, feel its rhythm, speak it, and enjoy its melody and rhyme. Poetry may be used with children in many ways: it may be read to them; they may speak it individually or in unison; they may write their own; either individually or as a group; they may read it silently and make selections to bring to class; and they may read it to one another. The use of poetry must not be formalized or its effect will be lost. To read a poem about snow without taking time, or having taken time, to observe, to really see, to talk about, and to laugh and think together of snow and the many things which might be associated with it, does not allow for the full force of the poem to be felt. A rigid teacher and a rigid classroom cannot use poetry successfully.

Group composition. The basic form of written expression in the primary grades is the group production. The teacher does the writing, usually on the chalkboard or on chart paper, as the children dictate what to write. This is usually done in connection with some group activity such as a trip, a project, a party, or a film. The composition might precede the activity—for example, writing the rules of behavior on a trip, or what to watch for in a film. Or it may follow as the recording of things seen, information the film gave, what happened at the party, or questions still to be answered. The emphasis is upon the children's composition; the teacher's writing is to relieve them of the pressures in handling the mechanics of the writing.

Compositions are improved if time is spent prior to the writing discussing what will be said, to what extent what is said must be arranged in some order, and some of the words to be used. This activity will lead to the discussion of the importance of organizing (i.e., outlining), the taking of notes to improve memory, and how to find the meanings of new words.

Group composition should precede individual composition of friendly letters, invitations, thank-you notes, news notices, and similar writing activities that primary children may engage in. These group compositions serve as models for later individual writing efforts. They may also serve as the basis for copy work in which children practice their handwriting and gain skill in capitalization and punctuation.

Dictated compositions. As children develop some facility in using manuscript writing and some knowledge of punctuation and capitalization items, the teacher may dictate short stories, reports, or summaries. The purpose of such dictation is to get children to listen for sentences and to think what the proper punctuation should be. Such practice also calls for the children to spell the words dictated.

This activity also begins with group composition. The class composes a story or report and the teacher writes it on the board. Attention is then called to the spelling of words that are new, the punctuation used, and the organization of the composition. Next, the children write each sentence, first repeating it after the teacher. Following the writing of each sentence, the teacher immediately inspects the children's papers to be certain the sentence has been written correctly. Any errors discovered are promptly discussed with the children concerned and corrected by them. This will ultimately lead to a later activity in which children will be able to write a dictated story that they have not previously seen.

Individual writing. Group composition leads also to individual composition. For some children this begins in the first grade, for others, the second. In all cases its successful achievement is largely dependent upon the skill that has been achieved in doing manuscript writing and the approach used by the teacher in helping the children with spelling problems. Of course, a deficiency in experiences to write about and a lack of knowledge about organizing a composition will also delay a child's success in individual endeavor.

Often in copying a group-composed letter, for example, individuality of expression may be encouraged. If a child has the ability to form letters without close teacher guidance, he may want to add his own "I miss you" or "My desk is by the door." The problem of spelling enters in, of course, and as an intermediate step the teacher may put several alternative phrases on the board for part of the letter, allowing each child to select the one he wishes to use.

Individual writing should always be done for a purpose. One purpose, of course, may be simply the enjoyment of achievement —what we call "creative" writing. More "practical" writing should also be done for specific purposes, the over-all purpose being communication. Letters written should actually be sent, thank-you notes delivered, summaries made because of an actual need to summarize, reports written to inform others, and blanks filled in because the information called for is really needed. Without genuine writing situations children will come to regard writing as merely a requirement rather than as a task done for a genuine reason. Conditioning against writing in the primary grades will have disastrous effects upon teaching attempts made latter.

Creative expression. Most creative language expression in the kindergarten and grades one and two is oral. Written creative efforts are largely group productions in which the teacher has done the actual writing—or in some instances the teacher will have done the writing for an individual child. Of course, as soon as children develop the ability to do manuscript writing, they may be encouraged to write and to be creative in this writing. The greatest handicap, then, is the spelling of the words they want to use. Usually this can be solved by the teacher's helping with the spelling. This procedure and others related to creative writing are discussed more fully in Chapter IV.

The goal in creative expression in the primary grades is not a finished poem or story, regardless of whether it is a group or an individual composition. The objective is to get real creative thinking from the children. In a sense this is the major objective of the language program in these grades and will be achieved, as has been previously suggested, by abundant opportunities for experiences with words and ideas and by provision for frequent occasions to be creative.

Mechanical limitations. The writing of the children in the primary grades is necessarily limited by their lack of skill in handwriting and spelling. The program of teaching these mechanical skills is presented in Chapter IV.

CHAPTER III

Instruction in
Speaking and Listening

In the sequential development of the language arts skills the child learns to talk and listen before he learns to read and write. A like progression has also characterized the historical development of language; man learned to speak with his fellow man before he learned to write and to read. When one gives thought to the use of language in present day-to-day activities, the importance of oral language is shown. Many authorities estimate that as much as 95 per cent of language usage is oral. The evidence is clear, therefore, that the school must concern itself with the teaching of oral language, developing the ability to speak effectively and to listen accurately and discriminately.

Objectives of the Middle Grades

To achieve any group of objectives, the primary ones should be attained first. A mountain climber does not attempt the sheer wall leading to the peak without first climbing the foothills. The teacher of the middle grades, therefore, should make certain that the pupils in his classroom have attained the objectives of the primary-grade oral language program before moving on to subsequent objectives. In the period from the third grade through the remaining years of elementary school for most children, however, emphasis in oral language instruction should be upon specific abilities and skills rather than upon spontaneity of expression and the other goals of the primary grades.

Basic to any oral language activities are the skills necessary for:

1. Careful articulation of speech sounds.
2. Distinct enunciation of vocal utterances.
3. Correct pronunciation of words.
4. Voice control, including volume, pitch, tone, and tempo.
5. Sensitivity to the needs, interests, and abilities of an audience.
6. Naturalness and sincerity of manner.

The development of these skills, however, will not result from efforts to teach them directly without attention to the context in which they are taught, no matter how carefully the program may be planned. True skill and ease in speaking can result only from genuine practice in all the various types of situations, or opportunities for speaking in which an individual child or adult naturally finds himself. Thus, direct instruction must be given in these special situations.

A more complete listing of the skills, knowledge, and abilities of which an elementary school child might reasonably be expected to have a fair mastery by the time he completes the sixth grade includes the following:

1. Speaking in a pleasant-sounding voice with careful enunciation and correct pronunciation.
2. Speaking with comparative ease before a group or with other individuals.
3. Speaking without the presence of annoying mannerisms, glaring errors in usage, and affectations.
4. Speaking with sincerity and clarity of meaning.
5. Knowledge of where to get material pertinent to a topic.
6. Knowledge of the elements that make a talk or a conversation interesting.
7. Listening with skill and courtesy as an individual or as a member of an audience.
8. Knowledge and ability in:
    a. Conversing about or discussing a topic.
    b. Telling a simple story interestingly.
    c. Telling an incident.
    d. Making a short announcement.
    e. Giving directions.
    f. Giving and returning greetings.
    g. Making and responding to introductions.
    h. Courteously asking and answering questions.
    i. Telephoning and answering a telephone call.
    j. Conducting a meeting.
    k. Giving and receiving compliments.
    l. Asking a favor with tact and courtesy.

Developing Good Speech Habits

Teachers generally recognize that oral communication is impeded by indistinct and careless utterances, faulty pronunciation, uncontrolled voice, and awkward manner. Some, however, fail to provide for direct attempts to improve speech, apparently assuming that children will outgrow these habits and practices.

Basic to making improvement is the identifying of errors and the habits and skills which need improvement. Often such identification can be accomplished through the use of a checklist and careful observance of each child's speech practices. The use of recording devices with which children can actually hear how they talk and note their own errors is invaluable. In addition, much may be accomplished by the children's hearing good speech. This latter sets for the teacher the task of making sure he articulates sounds distinctly, enunciates each syllable fully, and pronounces words naturally and acceptably. In addition, he must show ease, courtesy, and sensitiveness to his audience when he speaks.

Sometimes it is necessary for teachers to give specific training in the making of sounds, although it is better where there is persistent difficulty to bring the child to the attention of someone specifically trained in speech correction. Whenever a teacher needs to make a direct attack this procedure should be followed:

1. Show through illustration and demonstration how the sound should be made.
2. Have the child observe the position of the lips and the movement of the tongue in forming the sound.
3. Use a mirror so that the child may examine his attempts to imitate you.
4. After the child has made the sound correctly, have him practice it by repeating it several times, by speaking syllables and words which include it, and by speaking sentences in which the sound is used.[1]

Important also in the elimination of speech faults is the elimination of self-consciousness. While this is the major goal of the language program in the primary grades, many children come to the middle grades lacking assurance in speaking, lacking skill in controlling their voices, and retaining many errors in articulation, enunciation, and pronunciation. Genuine communication activities, if they are set in a classroom that is friendly and inviting, will do

---

[1] See speech texts such as Mardel Ogilvie, *Speech in the Elementary School* (New York: McGraw-Hill Book Co., Inc., 1954) or Charles Van Riper and Katharine Butler, *Speech in the Elementary Classroom* (New York: Harper & Brothers, 1955) for more specific suggestions.

much for developing both assurance and skill in speaking. Too, assurance in speaking may be helped if the children use some object or device to focus both their own and the audience's attention upon. Such things as pictures, cut-outs on a flannel board, charts or diagrams, the pantomiming of another child, films or filmstrips, and many other objects may be used by the speaker to build his confidence and to direct attention away from his face.

Basic Instructional Procedures

The child who has a genuine reason for writing or saying something has the best possible motivation for learning the needed language skills, as well as for continuing the correct use of them. The observant teacher will find many life activities created by the children in his class which may provide the basis for instruction in the language skills. At times the teacher will need only to help define for the children the real-life language situations that are present whenever humans are with one another. At other times the teacher may need to create language situations in the classroom which are similar to those outside the school. The genuineness of the language situation impels children to desire to improve their communication skills; language instruction dissociated from real communication needs is apt to be meaningless.

The intellectual and emotional climate of a classroom is of major importance in language instruction. The teacher, of course, has the major responsibility for the creation of this climate. The teacher who is sincerely interested in projects, problems, and class activities and who has the friendliness, patience, and faith to make each child feel at ease, confident of success, and free from the fears and tensions that normally block expression and learning will have the kind of classroom climate which best facilitates language instruction.

It is axiomatic also that no one can express more than he knows. A true language program makes provision for the *intake* of language as well as the *outgo*. Language expression, to be effective, must be based upon the reception of information, thoughts, and words through many rich and varied activities and experiences. Most adults know that they are likely to be embarrassed if they attempt to talk or write about something that is outside the realm of their experience, actual or vicarious. This fact needs to be kept in mind by teachers in planning their language programs.

Often the problem of intake is solved through the use of the curriculum's subject matter. In the fifth grade, for example, the children may be very interested in the westward movement of people in the early days of the United States. As the children investigate these hardy pioneers, the problems they encountered in travel, how they lived, and what the country they travelled through was like, they are motivated to read extensively, to study motion pictures and film strips, and to listen to stories and music. As a result of their efforts and interest they will have absorbed a considerable amount of interesting and useful information about the subject. It seems reasonable to assume that they would be able to express themselves more fluently on this topic than they would on some topic arbitrarily assigned and superficially studied in the language class.

While there are disagreements as to the extent of integration that should take place among the various school subjects, the fact remains that any subject area cannot be taught in complete isolation from others. This is particularly true for an area such as the language arts.

Adults generally recognize that language is a part of most human activities. The child, too, may soon come to realize the importance of language in all in-school and out-of-school activities in which he engages. The provision of lifelike activities and experiences demanding and motivating the use and mastery of the skills of expression will aid in the early creation of this realization. The child will perceive these skills as the tools by which he must receive and transmit ideas in connection with all of his daily activities. The content of these activities becomes the subject matter around which a successful language program operates. Such content may be the child's personal activities; it may be his particular interest in science; it may be a portion of the social studies unit on which the class is working; or it may be some home experience. The emphasis of a genuinely integrated language program is always upon the child's activities and experiences and upon the language needs which arise from these activities and experiences.

Since teachers are dealing, in a complete language program, with the content of expression and with freedom of the expression of this content as well as with the skills and techniques for making this expression most communicative, two types of lessons are generally called for. These may be called *expressional* and *correctional*. Expressional lessons deal principally with *what* is said rather than *how* it is said. The lesson focus is upon the purpose for the communication and the content of that communication. The correctional lesson, on the other hand, is derived from the expressional lesson. The purpose of the correctional lesson is to improve particular expressional skills that the expressional lesson has shown pupils to need.

Figure 1 shows the relationship between expressional and correctional lessons.[2]

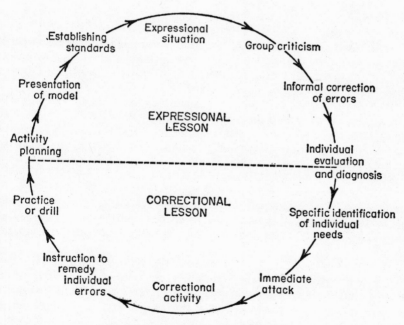

Figure 1. Language Instruction Cycle

---

[2] The instructional procedures suggested in this section are similar to those suggested in greater detail by the author and Harry A. Greene in *Developing Language Skills in the Elementary School* (Boston: Allyn and Bacon, Inc., 1959).

Expressional lessons. Natural situations occur for expressional lessons as children discuss plans for a science field trip, converse about an event that happened during the lunch period, tell a story they have heard or read, or introduce their parents to the teacher. These are genuine occasions for using the expressional skills and, as was suggested above, the emphasis on these occasions is upon the content rather than the form of the expression. This does not mean, however, that the lessons are unplanned, or that teaching techniques are not to be used. Some techniques useful in expressional lessons are the following:

1. Activity planning. Both teacher and pupils should know the purpose or purposes of the expressional activity. Much planning can be done together; this is particularly important at first, before the children have learned to select and organize their thinking about what they wish to communicate and how this communication may best be done.

2. Attention to the audience-speaker relationship. Planning is again called for in selecting content that the audience wants to hear and in recognizing that an attentive, interested audience is a strong motivational factor for the child doing the expressing.

3. Presentation of a model. Children learn language skills through observation, imitation, and practice. In order for a child to give an effective oral report, for example, he needs to observe and hear someone (usually the teacher) give a good report.

4. Establishment of standards. Standards should be set up for each expressional activity and these should be established by the pupils. The standards may be the outgrowth of observation of the model, criticism of a previous lesson, or discussion in planning the activity. The language of the standards should be that of the pupils; the standards should be written, and they should be retained so that they may be referred to.

5. Correction of errors. This will not be possible with all pupils since some will still be developing freedom and spontaneity in expression. A tactful teacher, though, will be able to correct many errors in usage and many bad speech habits promptly and without embarrassment to the child.

6. Criticism by the group. Frank and friendly criticism may be a part of many expressional lessons. The ability to criticize in positive ways, and without the cruelty that children sometimes show, needs to be taught. Again, the teacher is the model. The goal, of course, is self-criticism or self-evaluation; careful and constructive criticism of others will help a child see his own faults.

Correctional lessons. The object of a correctional lesson is derived from a genuine use of language—the expressional lesson.

The object might be the review of a skill that needs additional attention, it might be the introduction of a new skill, or it might be the practice of a desirable habit. In every case the correctional lesson should come directly from the children's expression, and it should follow the expressional lesson as quickly as possible. The following procedures are suggested for the effective use of correctional lessons:

1. Evaluation and diagnosis of expression. This step is necessary in order to identify specific errors, bad habits, or special language weaknesses to be worked on. The means of diagnosis will vary depending upon the language situation and upon the nature and refinement of the evaluative instruments available. Often, subjective evaluations of oral expression must be made based upon teacher-pupil judgments.

2. Identification of individual deficiencies. In order that the corrective lessons be directed toward the specific deficiencies of each child, the diagnosis must be as individual as possible. Perhaps each child, in relating his performance to the standards, can identify his needs. Self-evaluation and diagnosis is a strong motivator for improvement, but the evaluation must focus upon specific items, and those that most need improvement. Further suggestions on the identification of areas for improvement are made in Chapter VI.

3. Provision for immediate attack on deficiencies. A corrective lesson, in order to be effective, must follow the identification of specific errors or habits that need correction. Waiting a week or a month to work upon the needed skills removes the corrective lesson too far from the expressive lesson. Each corrective lesson must be specific and must take place the same day as the expressive lesson, if possible.

4. Work on individual errors. After children have identified their individual deficiencies, and instruction has been given in remedying those errors, they should be encouraged to discover for themselves the causes of the mistakes and to work on the ones they can correct.

5. Corrective practice. After children recognize the errors they have been making and learn how these may be corrected, properly designed practice must be provided in order to establish the new habit firmly. In oral expression this may mean that one child will practice his pronunciation with another child, a small group may practice a particular usage, or some may practice organizing their next reports. Often, the very proceeding to another expressional activity creates the needed practice.

Oral Expression in Specific Situations

Learning to speak in a communicative act is a process of utilizing the speech skills and the knowledge of what to say and how to say it in a situation which provides *experience* in using these abilities. The importance of experience in the development of oral language ability has long been recognized. Hatfield, in reporting to the National Council of Teachers of English in 1935, said:[3]

> Experience is the best of all schools. Certainly no one learns so thoroughly and few learn so rapidly, in any other. And experience need not be a dear school, if it is competently organized and is conducted by a capable teacher who illuminates each situation in prospect and in retrospect. . . . The school of experience is the only one which will develop the flexibility and power of self-direction requisite for successful living in our age of swift industrial, social, and economic change.

In order for the school to provide opportunities for the experiences needed to effectively develop oral expressional abilities, attention must be given to surveys and analyses of society's use of oral language. Such surveys and analyses have identified the situations in which oral language is used by adults and children. These are discussed in the following sections, with suggestions as to teaching procedures that may be used.

Conversation. Since conversation is generally regarded as the form of oral language expression of greatest social importance, it is deserving of much more instructional emphasis than the incidental attention frequently given in classroom. Presumably, many teachers believe that children have acquired sufficient skill in conversation prior to coming to school, that they will develop the skill as they encounter experiences in and out of school, or that skill developed in another oral language situation will be transferred to the children's performance in conversations. Too, conversation is a spontaneous activity based upon individual freedom of expression; such freedom of expression often leads to a "noise and commotion level" that some teachers fear. Teachers with these fears should recall how children learn language—the roles of imitation, habit formation, and practice—and the generally low level of conversational ability shown by their parents and teachers in normal conversational situations.

Conversation may be defined as an exchange of thought about one or more topics between two or more persons. The emphasis in

---

[3] *An Experience Curriculum in English.* A Report of the Curriculum Commission of the National Council of Teachers of English, W. Wilbur Hatfield, Chairman (New York: Appleton-Century-Crofts, Inc., 1935), p. 3.

such a definition is upon *exchange* and *thought*. Thus the qualities of a good conversationalist must include skill, ability, and knowledge in:

1. Thinking clearly.
2. Using English acceptably and effectively.
3. Speaking to the point.
4. Discussing without arguing.
5. Stimulating response from others.
6. Listening attentively and courteously.
7. Being interested in a wide range of subjects.

It is not the singular responsibility of the elementary school, of course, to develop good conversationalists; but it does have a responsibility, and certainly many opportunities. The school's program should begin in the kindergarten and primary grades and continue each year, with higher levels of development expected from grade to grade. Children have so many interesting experiences that no teacher should be at a loss in finding a basis for instruction. Throughout the school day many topics arise which are of interest to pupils and are related to the continuing purposes of the classroom program. The natural thing for pupils to want to do is to converse on these topics, and the wise teacher will exploit these situations.

At every grade level, however, children need wise guidance day by day if they are to attain the conversational ability desired and if full use is to be made of the situations which hold potential for teaching this ability. A well-planned program for teaching conversational skill should give attention to these principles:

1. Conversation is an exchange of ideas in turn between two or more persons who participate in the roles of listener and speaker.
2. Conversation involves genuine interaction about a subject of mutual interest rather than mere random talk.
3. Courtesy must prevail in the behavior of the participants even though the conversation may be very informal.
4. Conversationalists have the responsibility to be truthful and considerate in their remarks.
5. Good conversationalists avoid aggressive or argumentative attitudes.

In teaching conversation, attention should center principally upon the content of the conversation. Conversation generally has one to several objectives. Children must learn to stick to the point, or purpose, as they converse. This is not taught in a few lessons; it has to be developed over a period of years. This ability is actually a reflection of the individual's thought level; one must be able to hold his thinking to a purpose in order to talk with purpose. The same relationship is true for other aspects of the conversation content: total organization, relating details, and substantiating points of view. In spite of the fact that none of these abilities can be taught easily, they nevertheless can all be taught. For example, suppose a group of children are conversing about where they might store their art materials so that nothing will be damaged. In this conversation the purpose is to answer the question; this answer should be obtained first. However, as the conversation progresses, a teacher may divert the talk from the specific answer to aspects of the conversation itself. He may ask if any of the pupils have noted that some contributions are better than others and why this is so. Depending upon the age level, the children will in varying degrees respond and make points. One point might be that "Mike always has a good idea. He really sticks to the question." Another might be that "Jane always thinks of things that might happen if we put the art materials just anywhere." From such responses, the need for organization of thinking and sticking to the point, as well as other needs, may be shown. The next step would be to organize a conversation in which the abilities mentioned might be practiced.

From such an analysis, of course, specific speech-skill needs might be determined, items of usage needing correction noted, bad listening habits uncovered, and areas of deficiency in knowledge identified. The particular needs shown by the analysis will determine the type of corrective activity appropriate. Speech skills and usage may be practiced in almost any other oral expressional activity; organization may be improved through the organization of a written report; improving listening may call for a special lesson. In every case, though, the analysis should be a pupil-teacher one, should focus upon individual needs, and should lead to a correctional lesson as soon as possible.

Discussion. Discussion is quite similar to conversation but differs in that it has a more purposeful goal and a conclusion or agreement is usually reached. A conversation may have a purpose that is quite specific, as indicated above, but often this purpose is not stated. Before a discussion occurs there is generally a statement of the purpose. The teacher may say, for example, "We must discuss our behavior on the playground." In the lower grades, the purpose may be less obviously stated.

Discussion is also somewhat more formal than conversation and usually involves a larger group. A discussion needs a leader whereas in a conversation equal status is held by all participants.

Objectives held for the teaching of conversation and other oral language activities are appropriate also for discussion. The added ingredient which must receive major attention is that of establishing a definite problem. Whenever possible the determination of the problem should be the responsibility of the pupils. This will often be possible, as the problems discussed are those which arise naturally in the classroom: answering a specific question in social studies, planning a program, deciding an issue in classroom housekeeping, exchanging thoughts about an experience shared by all, and many others. For each pupil the teacher will want to develop the ability to:

1. State a problem clearly and concisely.
2. Hold his contributions to the topic.
3. Differentiate between fact and opinion and weigh each in forming a conclusion.
4. Adequately support statements made.
5. Discuss problems unemotionally with courteous recognition and acceptance of opposing viewpoints.

Leadership training is also an objective of discussion. Children need to be taught how to lead a discussion; how to open it, how to draw out information and points of view, how to summarize, and how to arbitrate sharp differences. Generally the best teaching in this area is accomplished through examples; the teacher as a discussion leader is the model.

The program suggested in the section on basic instructional procedures applies also to the teaching of discussion.

Storytelling. The telling of stories may be part of many other oral expressional activities; it may enliven a conversation, help to make a point in a discussion, or be used as part of a report—or even a telephone conversation. However, the principal concern here is the telling of stories as a separate language arts activity.

The language objectives of storytelling are similar to those in other oral expression, even though storytelling is primarily for enjoyment. In addition, storytelling calls for attention to the suitability of the content for the audience, to its organization, to the effects of word order and sentence construction, and to the mood created by the story itself and the teller's efforts. All of these indicate the need for a background of having heard many stories, well told, and having developed a real love for stories and the effective telling of them.

As in other oral activities, standards should be worked out by the pupils, with some direction from the teacher. Such standards as the following might be set up:

1. Know the story well and in proper sequence; do not memorize it, however.
2. Be able to "see" and "feel" the story. You must convey a mood to your audience, but you must know the mood yourself.
3. Tell the story in your own words and in your own way.
4. Use gestures, pauses, voice projection, and inflections which are natural to you and which add to the interest and effect of the story.
5. Speak directly to your audience.

These are not goals that the child can achieve easily, nor are they standards that should be observed in each storytelling activity. Only one or two should receive attention at one time; some may be achieved, of course, either incidentally or directly, through other activities of the language program. Too, storytelling should be for pleasure, and should occur naturally in a classroom whose climate is friendly and conducive to expression. Overemphasis upon standards may displace the pleasure aspect.

Effective storytelling by children is usually the result of the teacher's own love of stories and his successful telling of them to the children. The teacher is the model, a model who gets obvious pleasure in telling and listening to stories and instills this feeling in the children. The most important item for the teacher to consider is the selection of stories. A variety must be chosen—tales that fire the imagination, bring laughter, tell of adventure and daring, and portray beauty, courage, or understanding. Most should be relatively simple, without complicated plots—stories that children can themselves learn to tell.

Stories told by children do not always have to be presented to the entire class. Some may be told in small groups. Children may also practice in small groups before facing the entire class. Activities for grade three, for example, might include:

1. Retelling stories from readers or other books read.
2. Retelling stories the teacher has told or read to the group.
3. Drawing a picture and telling the story illustrated by the picture.
4. Making up stories to go with pictures found in children's magazines and books.
5. Giving the children three pictures of a four-picture story and having them make up the ending by drawing a fourth picture.
6. Taking turns serving as "story judge" to evaluate story presentations in terms of cooperatively developed standards.
7. Organizing a series of uncaptioned pictures into a story.

Activities for grade six might include:

1. Telling a story about an interesting experience the children have had.
2. Making up and telling about an experience they would like to have.
3. Telling "tall tales" and having children serve as judges to select the "tallest," the one best told, and so forth.
4. Telling favorite jokes and anecdotes.
5. Practicing "making a long story short."
6. Discussing standards and deciding upon those to be observed.

Dramatization. Dramatization is an oral language activity which springs from children's natural spontaneous play and their interest in hearing and telling stories. Dramatizations are planned activities ranging from those which are very flexible in pattern to those in which every detail of performance has been carefully worked out. Usually a dramatization is characterized by the presence of a written script, although many children's dramatizations occur on the spur of the moment, with no written guide prepared.

Emphasis in dramatization in the elementary school should be upon creativity. Children like to act: to give expression to a character, to pretend they are someone else, and to entertain others through their creativity. As children progress though the grades they become increasingly interested in exact dialogue, organizing the presentation—in short, doing a more thorough job. They will want to write dialogue, directions to characters, and other details of a script. Sometimes they will actually want to produce someone else's play for an audience. This activity is an important part of the dramatization program, but it usually follows a considerable period of practice, either without scripts or with those written by the children themselves.

Such situations as introducing people, answering the telephone correctly, delivering messages, and giving directions may also be dramatized. Much may be said also for the use of puppets and marionettes in dramatization. Children will often be less inhibited when they are hidden from an audience, and genuine creativeness may be shown by children performing behind the curtains of a marionette stage.

Reporting. This activity is an important one in the elementary school. In the lower grades it may include "sharing and telling" sessions; in the upper grades the reports are more formal and often deal with the the subject matter of social studies and science.

The giving of an oral report is similar in many ways to writing a report. In both cases attention must be given to the selection of appropriate material, the collection and organization of the material, and the presentation of the material to an audience. These abilities call for specific instruction in the following skills:

> 1. Selecting the topic, basing it upon the actual needs of the individual and the group; limiting its scope; and deciding upon pertinent questions to be answered.
> 2. Using reference sources in securing information (index, table of contents, dictionary, etc.); selecting information (note-taking, outlining, summarizing); and making note of quotes and the proper credit to be given for ideas and information.
> 3. Organization, including a good beginning and ending; simple outline; sticking to the topic; and attention to time limitation.
> 4. Presenting the topic; thinking about the physical conditions for presentation; and deciding what aids (charts, pictures, etc.) to use.

In addition to these skills the teacher will be concerned with usage and speech skills. These, and all of the skills suggested above, may be given attention by the pupils through previous evaluations of reports and by holding to standards established for preparation and performance. Teaching techniques are largely those of (1) showing the pupils how to use the index, how to take notes, how to write a summary, how to formulate good beginning statements, how to project one's voice, and so on; (2) having the pupil practice these skills; and (3) teacher-pupil evaluation of their performance.

Telephoning. Children usually come to school with some skill in using this essential medium of communication. Often, however, their skill extends only to the basic mechanics of placing and receiving calls; little knowledge is shown in the courtesies and the efficient use of the telephone. Generally, instruction in telephoning is relatively easy since children are naturally interested in technical devices and their use. They are also interested in dramatizing telephone situations.

Telephoning is an excellent way to use conversational skills, and to practice speech skills in general. Particular attention can be given to improvement of articulation, enunciation, and pronunciation. The children readily recognize the importance of developing clearness of speech when they must depend upon their voice alone to communicate. Considering the primary knowledge children have of telephoning, the chief school tasks are to:

1. Teach courtesy in giving and responding to messages, choosing times for using the telephone, and asking to use another's telephone.

2. Develop competency in opening and closing conversations, organizing messages to be given, placing calls, and receiving messages.

Interviewing. An important activity for the gaining of information that is increasingly being used in elementary and secondary schools is that of interviewing. An interview does not necessarily imply the questioning of one individual by another; the questioning may be of more than one person by more than one person. Thus, what we commonly think of as a conference—or perhaps a panel on TV—may be an interview; the purpose is to secure information through a process of questioning.

There are many natural opportunities for children in school to interview others. They may interview:

1. Parents about their special interests.

2. Community workers, such as firemen and policemen, about their work.

3. Professional people about their training.

4. The school principal about school policies.

5. A new child or teacher about his former home.

6. A classmate recently returned from a trip.

In teaching children to conduct interviews stress must be placed upon courtesy, careful planning of questions, ways of opening and closing, and sensitivity to time—i.e., appropriate time for appointments, the time being used for the interview, and the appropriate time to close an interview. These may best be taught through practice in actual situations and through dramatizing—or practicing for—actual interviews.

Meetings. While many meetings are largely taken up with the activities of conversation, storytelling, making of announcements, and general discussion, some are more formal and utilize parliamentary procedures. In these procedures both the leader and those participating in the audience need to know something about the meeting's conduct. Meetings of this sort occur frequently outside the school and many classrooms have clubs and room organizations.

The purpose of using parliamentary procedure is to conduct the business of the meeting in an orderly manner—a manner which respects the rights of all and which provides for the actual reaching of a decision.

The most important factor in conducting a successful meeting—and actively participating in a role other than that of leader—is a knowledge of parliamentary procedure. From such knowledge the children will learn to follow a set order of business: to properly make, second, and vote on motions; to be recognized before speaking; to keep records of meetings; and to recognize the role of discussion.

Giving announcements, directions, explanations, and so forth. The skills involved in these activities are, of course, similar to those in a number of other activities. A major skill to be attained, though, that is different from skills in some other activities is that of brevity. Brevity prompts particular attention to organization, clarity of expression, factors of interest, and the inclusion of all essential details. Superfluous details, distracting factors, and words and phrases which may be misunderstood must be culled out.

The teaching of skill and ability in these situations again is best done through real situations, of which there may be many each day. Children make announcements to the class, to other classrooms, and to the entire school about programs, events, games, lost-and-found items, and so on. Sometimes these announcements call for the giving of directions or explanations, an activity which almost everyone is occasionally called upon to perform. The giving of directions may also be practiced at school; for example, some children may fruitfully explain to others the proper way to leave the building in case of fire, to play a game, to conduct an interview, to move an action at a meeting, and others. Every possible opportunity should be utilized.

Choral speaking. Choral speaking is a group oral language activity. Often the speaking is done as a chorus; sometimes it is done in a succession of individual speaking roles; in every case a group of individuals is participating. Choral speaking is sometimes called choral reading, since the parts to be voiced may be read instead of given from memory.

Choral speaking has a number of values in improving oral expression. Perhaps the most important of these is the freeing of a child from the excessive shyness he might show when speaking alone. On the other hand, speaking with others requires that the overexuberant child respect the rights of others. In addition, choral speaking is good for improving enunciation, articulation, and pronunciation; for giving practice before an audience, as well as recognizing the importance of the audience in speaking situations; for improving listening; and for recognizing the importance of word arrangement in conveying meaning.

Basic to success with choral speaking ·is a background of experience on the part of the children, resulting from extensive listening to the teacher read and speak carefully selected prose and poetry. The actual steps in teaching a selection call for an impressive reading of the entire selection by the teacher, perhaps a rereading, a discussion of the mood or feeling the selection creates, and finally deciding how the group will read it: in unison, a-line-a-child, antiphonally, refrain (repeating a phrase at intervals) and others. Several ways may be tried before one is agreed upon as being best for the selection. A-line-a-child or refrain are usually easier to begin with; unison speaking generally calls for much practice.

Social conventions. Most language activities require the observance of social amenities since language is primarily used as a social instrument. Good manners and courtesy toward others should be a part of every oral expression situation. In addition to common matters of courtesy, children need special help in social situations which call for the conventions of (1) making an introduction, (2) responding to an introduction, (3) acting as a host or hostess, and (4) giving or responding to informal greetings.

There are many occasions in the school day when there is a real need to use one or more of these. Children may act as room hosts; they may introduce visitors to the class; they may extend and receive greetings from teachers, bus drivers, and others. Other occasions occur at home, at church, and at meetings children attend; the social conventions they use during these occasions may be practiced at school.

The Role of Listening in Oral Expression

The role listening plays in the communication process is being emphasized increasingly today after a period of much neglect. Listening is being recognized as a *receptive* language skill, an important way of gaining ideas and information, perhaps as important a factor in man's day-to-day communication activities as that of seeing.[4]

The importance attached to the listening skills has grown steadily since a survey make by Rankin of communication activities in the Detroit schools showed that 45 per cent of the time spent in communicating each day was devoted to listening, 30 per cent to speaking, 16 per cent to reading, and 9 per cent to writing. At the same time he discovered that the language arts instructional emphasis was on reading 52 per cent of the time; writing, 30 per cent; talking, 10 per cent; and listening, only 8 per cent. Later, Wilt discovered that children spend about two and one-half hours of the five-hour school day listening. Teachers estimated only half this amount.

Several factors account for the imbalance between need and instructional emphasis in listening. These are:

1. The overwhelming nature of the problem. We live in a virtual world of sound, are bombarded incessantly by useful and useless information, good and bad music, and the noise created by man's industry and tech-

---

[4] See Chapter 4 of *Language Arts for Today's Children* by The Commission on the English Curriculum of the National Council of Teachers of English (New York: Appleton-Century-Crofts, Inc., 1954) for a discussion of listening and its importance.

nology. The multiplicity of situations in which listening is done tends to cause perplexity as to how to attack the problem.

2. A continuing belief that since children enter school with some listening ability, little further teaching is needed. This same belief also influences the amount of instruction given in the speaking skills.

3. The difficulty of determining the actual skills needed in specific listening situations. This is largely a problem of measurement, one that is present in any activity as intangible and complex as listening.

4. Many teachers do not know how to give instruction in listening. The inattention generally given to the development of listening skills has been reflected in the teacher training programs; methods courses in the language arts often do not deal with listening.

5. The importance attached to the reading and writing skills tends to crowd out listening instruction in a school program. Teachers and the public alike are influenced by the fact that instructional effort toward improving reading and writing is more discernible than that focusing upon listening. Somewhat the same situation exists with respect to speaking.

6. The belief by many teachers that instruction in the various areas of the language arts can be given in a general language arts program causes the teaching to be too general and meaningless as to the development of specific skills.

Types of listening. A recent development in the attention being given to listening is the use of the term *auding.* Users of this term feel that "listening" is not comprehensive enough to describe the process.[5] The analogy is made with reading; reading is more than seeing and saying words. To read, one must see words, recognize them, gain meaning, and react to or make use of this meaning. To *aud* one must hear and listen with comprehension and appreciation, interpreting and making use of that which is heard. That *auding* will gain acceptance in describing the complete *listening* process seems doubtful.[6] Many classifications of types of listening have been made, which tend to define the listening act in the same manner that reading has been defined as consisting of overlapping levels of word identification, literal meaning, combining meaning with total experience, and reacting to what has been read through appreciation, inference, and critical evaluation. Some of the terms

---

[5] D. P. Brown, "Auding as the Primary Language Ability." Unpublished Ed.D. dissertation, Stanford University, 1954, p. 586.

[6] The April, 1961 issue of the *Review of Educational Research* on "Language Arts and Fine Arts" makes use of the term *listening* once again, after the 1958 issue had used the term *auding.*

used by certain authorities to describe special types of listening have been "appreciational," "informational," and "critical";[7] others have been labeled "attentive," "purposeful," "critical," and "responsive" listening.[8] The more accepted approach appears to be one of describing types of listening in degrees of increasing complexity of the act. Thus, the Commission on the English Curriculum defines the types of listening as "passive or marginal, appreciative, attentive, and analytical."[9]

Marginal listening is quite prevalent today, both in school and out. Such listening is strictly passive, with little or no apparent response. Listening to the radio or watching television often involves only marginal attention; similarly, in the classroom the child who stares fixedly at his teacher is usually hearing but not listening. In any marginal listening activity, a change in the situation— a different voice on the radio, the appearance of a favorite personality on TV, a sudden tone of warning from the teacher—may cause the listener to reach for another level.

Appreciative listening is done when the focus of the listener's thought is upon enjoyment. Listening to music, poetry, stories, and dramatizations is appreciational, although, again, a responsive chord may be struck which will cause the listener to become more attentive to and evaluative of what he has heard.

Attentive listening is done when close attention is given to the details of directions, announcements, introductions, and so forth. A response is often called for from this type of listening and the "mind set" needs to be different from that needed for appreciative listening.[10]

Analytical listening involves the higher skills of listening in the same manner that reading to evaluate or analyze involves the higher skills of reading. Speech that sets forth opinion, tries to sell something, attempts to sway or propagandize calls for analytical listening.

---

[7] Ralph G. Nichols, "Ten Components of Effective Listening," *Education,* 75 (January, 1955), 292–302.

[8] Earl J. Dias, "Three Levels of Listening," *English Journal,* 36 (May, 1947), 252–53.

[9] *Language Arts for Today's Children, op. cit.,* pp. 80–81.

[10] The issue of the effect of "mind set" is not resolved. Charles T. Brown in "Studies in Listening Comprehension," *Speech Monographs,* 26 (November, 1959), 288–94, reported no significant differences for different sets.

The listening skills. As has been suggested, the skills necessary for effective listening are closely related to those used in effective reading.[11] Both are receptive or "intake" activities needed to gain the information and concepts upon which speaking and writing may be based. Pratt and Greene have identified the specific skills within the framework of (1) perception of word or phrase, (2) comprehension of ideas or information, and (3) using understanding for further thinking.[12]

To perceive a word or phrase correctly when reading, one makes use of previous knowledge of words and uses the clues occurring in the word structure and form, phonetic knowledge, and the content itself, including accompanying visual aids. In listening, the listener tries to recall word meaning and deduces meanings of unknown words and expressions by listening to clues in the content. The process of perception in listening is perhaps more difficult in that re-listening is usually not possible in the same manner that re-reading is.

In the comprehension of ideas or information, the listener uses skill with which he (1) determines the main idea, (2) chooses the details, (3) organizes the ideas or information heard, (4) selects facts pertinent to a purpose, and/or (5) detects clues as to the direction of the speaker's thought. Again, the close relationship to comprehension skills in reading is apparent.

Using understanding for further thinking involves the skills of discovering relationships, recognizing emotive language, evaluating facts and points of view, and making inferences. These are the upper-level skills comparable to those needed to do analytical, critical, and creative reading.

Not all of the listening skills are needed in each listening act. Evaluative and inferential listening are not always necessary; there are times when we only need to "half-listen." At other times we need to listen attentively or with appreciation. In the development

---

[11] Edward Pratt and Harry A. Greene, *Training Children to Listen, A Monograph for Elementary Teachers,* No. 80 (Evanston, Ill.: Row, Peterson, & Company, 1955).

[12] For an excellent comparison of this relationship see David H. Russell and Elizabeth F. Russell, *Listening Aids Through the Grades* (New York: Bureau of Publications, Teachers College, Columbia University, 1959), pp. 6–7.

of real ability in listening, however, attention must be given to all of the skills.

Improving listening ability. Teaching listening, of course, must go beyond admonishing the children to pay attention and listen carefully. A program of instruction must diagnose needs, teach specific skills, and foster development of those skills. The responsibility of the teacher includes:

1. Making the children aware of the importance of listening. They need to learn that skillful listening is important at school, at home, and when they become adults. They must learn that listening skills can be developed; that their development results from the establishment of good habits.

2. Stimulating the sense of hearing, or auditory acuity, in the children. Children must become more "sound observant" and think about what they have "observed."

3. Providing abundant opportunities for meaningful listening. The opportunities provided must require listening for different purposes: for appreciation, for information, and for critical evaluation.

4. Teaching about the specific skills of listening and how each is used. This calls for specific teaching rather than merely giving attention to the superficial aspects of a skill.

5. Giving the children many opportunities to talk about things that interest them. The sharing of experiences, information, and ideas shows the genuine need for skill in listening.

6. Being a good listener and speaker himself. The teacher is the model for the children; how he listens, and what he expects of his listeners, are the characteristics they are likely to emulate.

In addition, there are general procedures useful in the teaching of listening. The most important of these is the building of favorable attitudes toward listening. This may be done by (1) showing the need for listening (children may record listening activities they engage in; records may be kept of the amount of time others— parents, teachers, custodians—spend in listening, or the kinds of situations they engage in which call for listening), (2) setting a goal or goals for each listening activity (the result of the listening should be of actual use), and (3) praising good listening performances. Other general procedures which should receive attention include:

1. Establishing readiness for listening through the recall of previous experiences and the discussion of the new vocabulary which will be heard.

2. Setting standards for listening experiences. These should be de-

veloped with the children and should focus upon the skills needing the most work.

3. Evaluating listening activities through group and individual check-lists.

4. Practicing courtesy in listening. Children should be made aware that all communication activities consist of interaction between speaker and listener—aware that good listening inspires a speaker and makes for better communication.

5. Using supplemental activities which help listeners organize their thinking and remember what they have heard. Instruction in note-taking, outlining, writing summaries, and using reference sources to check on the reliability of information heard are helpful aspects of listening instruction.

There may also be the need to use special lessons occasionally, each of which focuses upon a specific listening skill. For example, a time might be set aside for a listening lesson. For this lesson the pupils might be told that they are to listen for specific details in a selection read. The selection might then be read and the pupils examined either orally or by written test to determine how effectively they have listened.[13] Many listening exercises have been collected in the very useful publication *Listening Aids Through the Grades*.[14] These exercises, and those suggested in other sources, are helpful to a teacher endeavoring to build an effective program of listening instruction.

---

[13] Listening "lessons" have been suggested by: Robert Canfield, "A Study of the Effects of Two Types of Instruction on the Listening Comprehension of Fifth Grade Children." Unpublished doctoral dissertation, Syracuse University, 1960; and Margaret J. Early, "Suggestions for Teaching Listening," *Journal of Education, 137* (December, 1959) 17–20; and Ursula Hogan, *An Experiment in Improving the Listening Skills of Fifth and Sixth Grade Pupils.* Unpublished M.A. thesis, University of California, Berkeley, 1953; and Edward Pratt, *The Experimental Evaluation of a Program for the Improvement of Listening in the Elementary School.* Unpublished doctoral dissertation, State University of Iowa, 1953.

[14] David H. Russell and Elizabeth F. Russell, *op. cit.*

CHAPTER IV

Written Language Instruction

Written expression may be secondary to oral expression in terms of social importance but the specialized skills necessary for effective communication in writing demand a systematic instructional program. The differences between the two forms point up the deficiency in written expression, in that, unlike oral expression, it is not aided by the use of tone, inflection, accent, gesture, and the physical manner and appearance of the expressor. Written language must depend heavily upon certain mechanical skills to aid expression; it also comes under closer scrutiny than does oral language since it is recorded and can be reviewed. For these reasons, written language is probably regarded by most teachers as more difficult to teach than oral language. In spite of the prevalence of this belief, however, there are many factors operating which would suggest that such teaching should not be regarded as difficult. The principal one is the natural desire of children to write, which is another manifestation of their creative instincts.

Objectives of the Middle Grades

Children establish some facility in written expression in the primary grades, and near the end of the second grade many of them are able to write simple stories and letters. Keith's story is generally representative of normal achievement.

> On my birthday we went to the zoo.
> We saw the animals. They were fun to see.

Many of these children will have learned to spell several hundred words, to write in manuscript form with considerable legibility and speed, and to put their ideas into writing with clarity and order. However, many others are much less mature. Hence, the principal elements of effective written expression are developed in the middle grades. Language instruction even in later years consists of refining the development that largely takes place during the time spent in

48

the middle grades; for some children, of course, the facility developed in these middle grades remains essentially the same throughout their lives. Objectives of the written language program for these grades may be outlined as follows:

1. Development of ability and skill in the mechanical aspects of written expression, such as in:
    a. Spelling.
    b. Handwriting.
    c. Form or appearance.
    d. Punctuation and capitalization.
2. Development of abilities in the use of written language in the specific situations, such as:
    a. Letter writing.
    b. Outlining and note-taking.
    c. Filling in forms.
    d. Writing reports, memoranda, and minutes.
    e. Writing notices, labels, and titles.
    f. Writing directions, rules, and announcements.
3. Development of ability and interest in creative writing.
4. Development of skill in:
    a. Using sources of information.
    b. Proofreading and self-editing.
5. Development of the grammatical and rhetorical skills (i.e., usage, sentence sense, clarity, and organization) which are useful to both written and oral expression.

In each of the above areas there are more precise objectives which must be achieved before development of skill in the general area takes place; these are discussed in later sections of this chapter.

The Instructional Approach in Written Expression

It is true in the teaching of written expression that "children learn to write by writing." No amount of instruction in mechanics and in grammar and usage will accomplish what daily writing for genuine purposes will. As a publication from the United States Office of Education states:[1]

> Children learn to write by writing. There should be opportunities for every child to write every day in ways that are purposeful. This will not be writing of a formal sort, but rather for many purposes:

---

[1] Helen K. Mackintosh and Wilhelmina Hill, *How Children Learn to Write,* Bulletin 1953, No. 2, U.S. Department of Health, Education, and Welfare (Washington, D.C.: Government Printing Office, 1953), pp. 10–11.

writing a question on the board, taking notes to answer questions on a problem, writing directions for going on a trip, keeping a record of the weather, writing a letter, ordering merchandise, making an outline for a play, making a bibliography of books containing stories about dogs, writing a fanciful story, or any one of a hundred or more activities that children find interesting and useful.

Teachers should have no difficulty in stimulating most children to want to write. Children will write when the writing is done for a purpose that is apparent to them and that has developed because of some experience which has shown them a need for communicating with others. One author tells of a third-grade teacher who has her pupils write a story each school day, an assignment which certainly reflects an emphasis upon writing.[2] However, he does not report the children's understanding of this activity. Do they see a purpose in it? Is the purpose theirs, or is it their teacher's? Answers to these questions are crucial to writing instruction. When children have reasons to write that they understand—and they understand the communication act—they will have the best purpose possible to learn the writing skills in the first place, as well as for continuing to practice them. The key to all suggestions for teaching written expression is the genuineness of the need for writing. One group of teachers has stated:[3] "Ever since we began expecting children to write only when they had a genuine need or the earnest desire to do so, we have found them eager to write well. In that mood they have been sensitive to our guidance and suggestion."

By the time children have progressed to the middle grades in the elementary school they have had many experiences and have developed many interests. Without doubt there are great numbers of things about which they could write. However, the problem is not that simple. Teachers should not assume that further opportunities for experiences do not have to be provided. Neither should they assume that activity provides experience—at least not always the experience one may be inclined to assume or hope for. Activities that are provided should lead to children learning many things that they want to tell others about; the activities must show the children

---

[2] Don M. Wolfe, *Language Arts and Life Patterns* (New York: The Odyssey Press, Inc., 1961), p. 6.

[3] Alvina Treut Burrows *et al., They All Want to Write* (Englewood Cliffs, N.J.: Prentice-Hall, Inc., 1955), p. 3.

that others may not know what they have learned and will want to share this knowledge. The purpose of the activity must be known to and be meaningful to the children.

As has been suggested in Chapter III concerning the development of oral language skills, two types of lessons are necessary to bring about adequate mastery of the essential expressional skills, the expressional and the correctional. The description of these two types of lessons given in Chapter III applies to similar lessons in written expression. These lessons should form the basic procedure used; modification and expansion of them are suggested in the following sections.

Developing written expression in specific situations. Writing is used for specific purposes; most writing is done in situations which are of a communicative nature. We write a letter to tell a friend what we have been doing or to reply to a business inquiry; we make an outline to help us organize a talk; we fill in the blanks in our income tax forms; we write a notice for a bulletin board advertising something we have for sale; and we write the minutes of club meetings because an account of activities helps keep the club functioning. In these situations specific skills and abilities are necessary to produce effective expression. It is the purpose of this section to describe the most important of these situations; to identify the skills, abilities, and knowledge needed; and to suggest appropriate teaching procedures.

Letter writing. There is probably rather universal agreement that the most important written language activity any of us engages in is letter writing. At some time or other everyone needs to write a friendly letter, an informal social note, or a business letter. The school's instructional program must include the writing of letters of all types and must deal with matters of form and appropriateness in each case. Letter writing is most effectively taught when it is an integral part of a naturally occurring activity within the classroom. Again, there is no need to search for artificial situations which force the writing of letters. Children will thus better understand the need for a particular type of letter and what matters of content, form, and courtesy are important. The following list, suggesting many forms of letters, only partially indicates the many real occasions where letter writing may be done:

1. A *friendly letter* or postcard to another class, another school, a former classmate, last year's teacher, or a student in a foreign land.

2. A *thank-you* letter to a parent for showing pictures to the class, to friends and relatives for presents at Christmas, to members of another class for the use of some books, to someone in the community for the loan of materials, to the custodian for some special favor.

3. An *invitation* to parents to come to a program, to another class or school to exchange visits, to the principal or supervisor to observe an activity.

4. A *reply* to an invitation to visit another classroom, to visit a parent's home to see a collection of relics, or to city officials to tour the city hall. The reply may either accept the invitation or express regret at not being able to do so.

5. A *sympathy* letter to a sick classmate or teacher, or to a teacher or the family of a classmate after a death or an accident.

6. A *greeting* to other children or classes in the school on a holiday; to the principal, teachers, cafeteria workers, or others on birthdays; to various friends on special occasions.

7. A *request* to a company or an individual for information, to a chamber of commerce or a business for materials, to a business-man for permission to visit his business, or to the principal for permission to take a trip.

8. An *application* for a position on the school paper or year-book, for a job in the school office, for summer work, or for an after-school job.

9. An *order* to a business firm for class supplies or books, or one for a magazine subscription.

These are only a few of the many possible situations that would call for the writing of letters. An alert teacher, keeping the principle in mind that letters written as a natural part of a class activity will be the most effective procedure to use for teaching letter writing, will think of many more occasions.

As has been stressed above, every letter should be written for a purpose. The purpose from one type of letter to another, as well as from one individual letter to another, will vary. Attention to content is always important. At every grade level the teacher and the children should spend time discussing the purpose or purposes of the letters that are to be written. Proportionately, more time must be spent upon this in the primary grades, of course, than in the middle or upper grades, as older children will more easily recognize the purposes. In all cases, however, the more genuine the occasion for the letter writing the more easily the purpose will be understood. Furthermore, even when the children have a general idea of the need for a letter or letters, and some notion as to what should be said, the periodical discussion of content and its organization is helpful.

In addition to discussion of the contents of particular letters, class efforts at improving organization, phrasing of thoughts and information, and decisions as to details to be included, other suggestions for teaching attention to content in letters are:

1. Analyzing letters the class or individual pupils have received as to their organization and whether or not they have effectively communicated.

2. Encouraging pupils in the upper grades to plan what they want to say, possibly by an outline or the making of notes, before beginning the writing.

3. Helping the children to think of words and phrases which might be used instead of the somewhat trite ones commonly used in letters.

4. Having the children exchange letters they have written for the others' analysis.

5. Reading letters to the class that are interesting and well-organized.

Matters of form are, of course, of secondary importance in letter writing instruction. This does not mean, though, that form does not have to be taught. Most textbooks contain samples of different types of letters and these give attention to the details of form. Unfortunately, a letter reproduced on a printed page in a book has a different appearance than would that same letter in the original. The size of the paper, the widths of the margins, the lengths of the lines, the spacing for indentations and between lines, and other factors tend to distort the model. To supplement a textbook model a teacher should develop with the class a letter form using content dictated by the children. Following class acceptance of the form and content, each child should produce a model letter for his personal reference use. Similar models may be prepared later for other types of letters and for envelopes.

Courtesy in letter writing should also be included in the instructional program. Many courtesies appropriate to this expressional activity are also appropriate to others and may have an unknown amount of carry-over throughout a child's life. Courtesy, also, is best taught when the expression is sincere. As the teacher guides informal discussion and utilizes real situations, the children become sensitive to the importance of showing courtesy to the reader of a letter. Courtesies which should be taught include the following:

1. Letters should be answered and mailed with relative promptness.
2. Letters should be carefully read for errors in content, usage, and spelling before mailing.
3. Another's letter should not be read except upon request.
4. Questions should be answered when they have been asked.
5. Expressions of congratulations, sympathy, good wishes, and respect should always be made sincerely, and when they are appropriate.
6. A stamped and addressed envelope should be enclosed when one is requesting a reply from an unknown person or from one whom would not ordinarily respond to such a request.
7. One should use appropriate materials (pen, paper) and aid the reader by writing neatly, with adequate margins and straight lines.
8. Letters should not be written in anger.
9. In a typed letter the signature is both written and typed.

Outlining. The making of an outline occurs in two types of situations. In one an outline is made to help organize one's thinking after reading or listening to a statement. In the second type of situation the outlining is also done to help organize one's thinking, but this time before making an expression. Outlining is a necessary aid to effective study and learning, and as such should be included in the language instructional program of the elementary school.

Outlining instruction begins in the kindergarten and other primary grades with the introduction of the ideas of classification and organization. The kindergarten teacher may write on the board the procedure the class will follow in going on an excursion: how to march to the bus, how to sit, how to get off the bus, what to look for, and so forth. Such organization or listing will not be identified to the children as an outline, nor will it be in the customary outline form, but the basic principle of outlining is present. This is the principle that needs to be repeatedly brought to the attention of children: outlining has no purpose other than to aid in clear and orderly thinking.

In the other primary grades children should learn, and should practice, arranging ideas in proper sequence, finding the main topic of a paragraph or longer selection, putting material under proper headings, and selecting important details relative to a topic. They should also learn the basic form for an outline consisting of a main topic or title and the main headings. This should include the capitalization of the Roman numerals, the placing of periods after the numerals, and the placing of periods after the main headings *if* they are in sentence form.

In the intermediate and upper grades instruction in outline form and use needs to continue. Headings are further divided, and the form for this must be taught. There is no single acceptable form for an outline; textbooks used in language classes generally make specific suggestions, however. Useful principles to follow for all instruction in a particular school are the following:

1. Each outline should have an introductory and a concluding topic fragment or sentence.
2. Major topics should be of comparable importance.
3. Each major topic should be directly related to the outline subject.
4. At least two sub-topics are necessary under each major topic.
5. Consistency in numbering, lettering, indenting, capitalizing, and punctuating should be maintained throughout an outline.
6. Outlines may be in either sentence or phrase form. If they are in phrase form no punctuation is used after the topics. Both are equally correct, but the form should be consistent throughout a single outline.

Outlining should always be taught as the need for more careful planning for expression or for retention of information arises. When it is taught it must be taught thoroughly and frequent use must be made of it for genuine purposes. Stress should be upon the point that tasks worth doing are worth planning for in advance and that outlining is valuable in any expressing that the child wants to do well.

Reporting. The writing of reports does not assume the importance as a language activity outside of school that it does in the school. Certainly in the elementary school there are few writing tasks that are done more frequently. Included in this topic, in addition to the usual one of reporting information on a topic, are book recommendations and reports, summaries of records and experiences or things read, and written directions and accounts.

In one classroom, Billy wrote a report to be put on the bulletin board which told of the work of the control tower operator at the airport; Mary wrote directions for the class on how to use the index of a book to find information on a topic; Rex wrote an account of *What Does a Jet Pilot Do;* and Virginia summarized what her father and mother had told her about their flying experiences. These, and many others which were written, show how in studying a single social studies unit—this one was on transportation in the United States—unlimited opportunities for writing reports occur.

Even in the kindergarten and first grade, children begin giving reports—oral ones—and also begin dictating to the teacher their thoughts and knowledge. In the second and third grades written reports and summaries may be made by the children themselves. The objectives for an instructional program in report writing should be similar to the following:

PRIMARY GRADES

a. To begin to use pictures and stories to report observations.
b. To learn to be accurate in observing and reporting.
c. To develop ability in noting essentials clearly and in order.
d. To learn the importance of definite, descriptive language.
e. To learn to be persistent in tasks of long duration.

INTERMEDIATE GRADES

a. To prepare reports of increasing length and complexity.
b. To learn the importance of advance planning for reporting.
c. To learn the use of key words to help recall data afterwards.
d. To develop the habit of noting the source of material and giving credit for its use.
e. To learn care in selecting appropriate material and transferring it accurately.

UPPER GRADES

a. To extend and refine previous objectives.
b. To acquire skill in taking notes.

Emphasis in the teaching of reporting should be upon communication. Children will regard reporting as a natural thing to do when the topic to be reported is one of personal interest and when they are confident that there will be an audience to read the report.

Filling in forms. As a form of written expression the filling in of forms does not constitute a major area, especially in terms of the volume of words used, but it does represent an important activity. Both adults and children are frequently called upon to record information accurately in blank spaces. Usually these situations are rather crucial ones. Children fill in the information on test booklets and school information sheets. Adults must put the necessary information on applications for drivers' licenses, on order blanks, or on income tax reports. In the classroom every possible situation should be utilized to teach children to fill out forms neatly, accurately, and completely. Specific items which may be used include the following:

1. Enrollment cards.
2. Library loan cards.
3. Library call slips.
4. Test booklets.
5. Deposit slips for school savings accounts.
6. Savings withdrawal slips.
7. Subscription blanks for magazines.
8. Order forms for books or materials.
9. Money order forms.
10. Permission forms for parent's signature.

Announcements, notices, labels, titles, and signs. Activities dealing with these forms of written expression are constantly occurring in the elementary school. All of these activities call for the writing of short, concise statements or phrases. The emphasis is upon this conciseness and upon neatness and accuracy. The principal of one school helps his teachers by fostering this kind of writing through the maintenance of a bulletin board for notices the children post. Everything posted is screened for conciseness, clearness, and accuracy by a committee of upper-grade children and a teacher. The members of the committee and the responsible teacher are changed several times a year and the children consider membership on the screening committee an honor for which to strive. The following are several items of one day's posting:

Lost: A small brown dog named Snap. He looks mostly like a terrier. *Sammy Himes, Grade 4*

Do you want to play ball? There will be a Little League meeting Monday, April 12, after school. It will be in Miss Jenk's room. *Bill Sloane*

Help! My mother wants a sitter for Saturday. I'm nine years old but my little brother is only five. The sitter would have to be about twelve. *Sue Fischer, Miss Hunt's room*

Of course, there are many opportunities in the classroom for writing titles for posters, pictures, and displays and for labeling many things. In addition, these suggestions may be helpful:

1. Precede the writing with oral discussion. Have the children practice giving an announcement, stating a title, or suggesting a sign before attempting to write them.

2. During the oral discussion attention should be directed to appropriateness of wording. Looking at and discussing announcements, notices, and so forth as the basis for thinking about the words to be used is helpful.

3. Get the children interested in noticing signs, labels, and notices in stores, along highways, in newspapers, and on bulletin boards. Suggest the practice of rewriting the weak ones they discover.

Records and minutes. Children need to keep records on such things as the growth rate of plants, weather conditions, effects of certain dietary conditions on animals, their own progress in learning something, the books they have read, and the contributions of the class members to the science table. Sometimes these records may amount to only a mark, a number, or a date; at other times the records may include sentences or short paragraphs. In any case attention must be given to accuracy, regularity, and the legibility of the record.

The minutes of a club represent another type of record. Most classrooms will have at least one club for which records must be kept and often there may be several. Also, class committees of a temporary nature may need to keep records in the form of minutes of the committee meetings.

Suggestions made in other sections of this chapter relative to other forms of written expression also apply here. Again, the emphasis is upon writing where expression is actually needed.

Rules, receipts, and memoranda. There are many occasions for the writing of rules for games, making objects, and procedures to be observed, such as leaving the building in case of fire. Receipts may be written for materials returned, for monies given to a pupil acting as treasurer for a party, and for other similar situations.

Memoranda may be written as reminders of things to be done, of materials to be brought from home or to be purchased, and of items related to a topic. In the writing called for in any of these situations, emphasis again should be upon accuracy—upon the inclusion of all necessary detail. The teaching procedures are those suggested in preceding sections.

Note-taking. Related in some aspects to several of the previously described writing activities is that of note-taking. The taking of notes, especially, is a preliminary activity to further writing. As children go on social studies trips, conduct science experiments, and look for information relative to some subject they have occasion to take notes. The notes may then serve as the basis for the writing of reports, summaries, or records. Note-taking is similar to outlining in that it does not represent an end in itself but is helpful in the preparation of final written product.

Note-taking that is of genuine value is something that is not learned incidentally. The development of skill in note-taking may begin in the kindergarten and first grade as the teacher writes lists of things to watch for on a trip, things seen on the trip, and things to be remembered. Primary children may draw pictures which show their understanding; they may dictate descriptive labels; they may find pertinent passages. These activities, and many others, are the beginning of note-taking. In the middle grades children may write notes as they observe, listen, and read. In this writing they will need to be helped to write only the important facts, to abbreviate words when possible, to write legibly, and to be sure they have written enough to be useful later.

Accuracy in taking notes from written sources must be stressed, along with the idea that the taking of notes is not copying. Children should understand that sometimes the copying of someone else's words is appropriate but that when this is done they must be sure to give credit to the writer.

Bibliographies and footnotes. Children in even the lower elementary grades should understand the necessity, as mentioned above, of giving credit for information and ideas. In written reports and summaries accurate reference to the sources of material should be made. Often the material is of a general nature and the inclusion of a bibliographical reference is sufficient, but at other times more precise reference may be appropriate and a footnote may be used.

Bibliographical and footnote form should always be appropriate for each grade level. In the lower and middle grades, the listing of the name of the author and the name of his work is usually adequate in a bibliography. In the upper grades, details as to the publisher may be added. As for footnotes, in the middle grades a simple note such as *"First Book of Stones,* page 8," is sufficient. Again, in later grades more may be added. The form to follow for both footnotes and bibliography should be one of those suggested in language textbooks or those agreed upon by the teachers in a school as standard forms.

Fostering Creative Writing

Creativity may be found in many activities, including many occurring in schools. In schools we have long recognized creativity in various forms of art—music, painting, sculpture, and dance; only recently has much attention been given to creative expression in areas often thought of as routine. Along with teaching in others of the three R's, language instruction is often considered somewhat routine and little attention has been given to creativity, particularly in the elementary school, until recently.

The teaching of creative expression in language, specifically that of creative writing, is a matter of some controversy. Some writing authorities, usually college teachers of English, hold that the teaching of creative writing should not be attempted before college, and that such instruction even then should be limited to students showing considerable writing talent. Other authorities, including many concerned with elementary education, claim that creativity cannot actually be taught but that it may be encouraged and that the result of such encouragement may be writing that is creative. Still others hold that children may be taught to improve their writing to such an extent that the result, if not actually creative, will show some of the elements of creativity in its sparkle and interest.

There are differences, too, in definitions of creative writing (other than those implied in the above). Some writers, considering procedures in elementary school language arts instruction, distinguish between writing that is "practical" and that which is "creative." The basis for this position is that elements of form and mechanics must be observed in "practical" writing, while they need not be observed in "creative" writing. These writers hold that creative writing should be done primarily as natural and spontaneous expression and not for an audience; that giving attention to mechanics and form will repress creativity.[4]

The point of view in this monograph is that all children's expression may be improved, that in order for the maximum improvement to take place teaching is necessary, and that what is commonly termed "creative expression" does not necessarily lack practical value and purpose. Further, the use of language in all situations other than that of merely repeating the words of another is actually creative, though lacking as such expression may be in the imagination and vitality we seek. It may be spontaneous, and even show imagination and sparkle, and yet be the parroting of another. Creative expression perhaps may best be defined here by a consideration of the purpose for teaching it: to encourage children to (1) use language that is their own, (2) express because of a real desire and feeling of purpose or need, and (3) make the expression different from the commonplace and unimaginative.

Creative language may take many forms. It may appear in a letter, in a report, in the minutes of a meeting; it may be a poem, a story, a play; and it may be either oral or written. Creative expression may be as practical as an announcement attempting to recover a lost article. On the other hand it may be as lacking in immediate utility as an entry in a personal diary. In all cases, though, the elements of the individual's own words, production without compulsion (not necessarily without assignment), and some departure from commonplace language make it creative.

The teacher's responsibility. It probably is true that creative expression cannot be taught in the sense that addition is taught. On the other hand, it may be equally true that it may be taught in the sense of setting the stage for learning, as in learning to appreciate literature or music. This form of teaching calls for increasing the awareness of pupils, providing opportunities to gain and retain thoughts, helping store up ideas and information, and releasing expression in a climate of encouragement. Creative expression doesn't

---

[4] See, for example, Mildren A. Dawson and Marian Zollinger, *Guiding Language Learning* (Yonkers-on-Hudson: World Book Co., 1957). The expression of this point of view is best developed by Alvina Treut Burrows, *et al., They all Want to Write* (Englewood Cliffs, N.J.: Prentice-Hall, Inc., 1952).

"just happen." It doesn't "just happen" with the truly talented and creative adult writer, and it will not "just happen" for a child in the classroom. Preparation must be made. The following steps suggest the setting of the stage—the teaching—that usually needs to be done.

1. Development of classroom and school communities that are friendly, leisurely, warm, honest, and appreciative of the personalities of all. The personality of the teacher usually creates this atmosphere; the teacher is the key for a particular class. The principal, the bus drivers— even the clerks—must help, however. The classroom and school must also be physically attractive.

2. Provision of many opportunities for absorbing knowledge. There is no end to possibilities here; certainly many stories of all types must be read, poetry must be read, time must be taken to appreciate the little things together, experiences must be talked over with children, and interest must be built in expressive and apt words and phrases. Of course, a room filled with books, thought-provoking objects, and challenging activities is vital.

3. Doing much oral expression of all types, but particularly those that call for considerable organization of ideas such as oral reporting and storytelling. Dramatic play and other forms of informal dramatization should be encouraged. The teacher must tell many stories to establish the foundation for the children's storytelling. The teacher's recording of group and individual stories, records, poems, and reports is also important. All of these activities are vital as preparation for beginning creative writing but they should also continue after the writing has begun.

4. Recording ideas, picturesque words and phrases, words which create sensory impressions, and interesting topics. Group recording of these may be done on charts and hung about the room; individual children may keep lists in notebooks. Collecting pictures, talking about them, and deciding upon titles is also helpful.

5. Getting started with writing, and doing an abundance of it. Appreciate the writing that is done, but make the expression of appreciation honest. Establish situations which not only allow for writing and foster it but often require it. Provide for such things as a "quiet hour," a writers' corner, a writing time, and so on, with a flexible enough schedule to be able to take advantage of special occasions.

6. Begin to teach techniques of how to devise a plot, how stories may begin, how to build up to a climax, how to keep out unnecessary details, and how to include characterization and description. A start on this may be made, for example, by finding stories that have different beginnings. Make use of the pupils' knowledge of outlining and the accuracy that has been shown in record keeping. If a pupil does not understand the

purpose of an outline, and is unable to use it, there is little reason, of course, to expect much success with the teaching of other organizational and rhetorical skills.

7. Teach proofreading for errors in mechanics and usage. This step comes after the pupils have developed genuine interest in writing and have experienced some success with it. It may not always be the last step but certainly must come after the motivation is present.

Creativeness and correctness. As mentioned above, many authorities on creative expression stress that attention to correct language and mechanics may retard creativeness. Various interpretations have been made of this theory. It certainly is true that correctness of mechanics and acceptable language do not necessarily mean good expression. It is also true that emphasis in writing or speaking should always be upon the content of the expression rather than upon matters of form. On the other hand, correct usage and mechanical skills are so interwoven with content in the total product of normally satisfactory expression that it is impossible to separate completely one from the other or to say that one is of such importance that no regard need be given to the others.

Children who develop a real feeling for expression, who feel that they have something to say, and who know that there is a purpose for their expression, will want to use acceptable language and form. Most children, as most adults, when concentrating upon the ideas they are trying to express, are not concerned with particular words and items of form. However, children, again like adults, will later correct errors and rewrite as seems necessary. This practice places emphasis upon content first, but also does not disregard mechanical elements of the expression. Of course, for the correction to take place the pupils must have learned how to proofread and must have knowledge of, and have practiced, the essential mechanical skills and usage items.

Developing the Mechanical Skills

For written expression to be completely effective attention must be paid to matters of mechanics and convention. The way expression is written must aid communication rather than distract from it. Errors in spelling, illegible handwriting, and improper capitalization and punctuation distract the reader of a selection from the thought itself. Such distractions interfere with communication and

must be avoided. Children in the elementary school must be made
to understand this fact; attention in teaching to these mechanical
skills will aid that understanding.

Spelling. Ability to spell correctly is clearly needed by children
in order for them to carry on their school work successfully and as
preparation for their later study and work. There is a need for
spelling each time a child or adult writes something; for most, this
need is a daily one. In the majority of instances, for writing to
communicate effectively the words must be spelled correctly. To do
less may lead to misinterpretation of what has been written. Certainly, negative judgments are made of the writer by his readers if
his spelling ability is poor. The occurrence of such judgments may,
in itself, cause the writing to be less effective as communication.

All elementary schools give some attention to spelling in their
curriculums. For most, the spelling program centers around a spelling textbook or workbook in which words are given and exercises
provided that are designed to teach the children to spell those words
and to develop ability in spelling other words they will need to write.
Other schools make their own spelling lists, and a few teach spelling
only incidentally. In general, however, the schools' spelling programs perform only a part of the task necessary for teaching children to spell correctly in all their written work. Attempts to remedy
this have led to programs which correlate spelling instruction with
other curricular areas. These attempts often are not really successful
because of the artificiality of much of the correlation. Schools that
effectively teach children to spell teach an attitude of concern for
correct spelling as well as a basic core of words that are highly
useful in writing. The key is not correlation or integration of curricular areas but a focus upon these two goals. When this is done,
the children learn to spell the words they most often write and also
make efforts to spell all words correctly.

In selecting words to be taught attention should be given to research on words most frequently written by children and adults.
This practice has been followed for the selection of words in most
commercial spelling books, although in too many such books some
have been included which are seldom written, the excuse for their
inclusion being that they teach certain phonetic principles. There is
considerable fallacy in this, however, in that few phonetic principles
apply in spelling. In situations in which a school selects its own

words the lists are often overweighted with local words and words from other curricular areas, such as social studies, even though such words actually may be infrequently written. The safest practice to follow is to select the most commonly written words as reported in studies—for example, those by Horn, Rinsland, and Fitzgerald. Horn shows that 2000 words and their repetitions make up about 95 per cent of the words written by adults.[5] Rinsland reports similar figures concerning children's writing.[6] Other studies, including Fitzgerald's, have shown that about 2500 words account for approximately 90 per cent of the words used most frequently by children and adults.[7]

Emphasizing the teaching of a carefully selected core of words should not be taken to mean that no other words should be taught, nor that no other words will be learned. Adjustment of the basic list should be made for the differing needs of both slow and gifted learners. Also, in some instances there may be a need to learn to spell some words from a social studies or science unit, depending upon whether writing is to be done, and if children are to learn to write effectively they must certainly write often, and about things which are of interest. Generally, however, as an attitude of concern for correct spelling is developed, these words will be correctly spelled in written work even though they may not have been formally taught or permanently learned.

Two plans for the teaching of spelling have been developed and frequently described. These are the *test-study* and the *study-test* plans. Research evidence clearly favors the test-study procedure, which identifies specific learning tasks for each pupil.[8] Arguments for the study-test procedure generally emphasize the need to develop word meanings before learning to spell the words. This argument is largely nullified if the words selected are those most frequently written. The test-study plan consists of the following:

---

[5] Ernest Horn, *A Basic Writing Vocabulary: 10,000 Words Most Commonly Used in Writing.* Monographs in Education, No. 4 (Iowa City: State University of Iowa, 1926).

[6] Henry D. Rinsland, *A Basic Vocabulary of Elementary School Children* (New York: The Macmillan Company, 1945).

[7] James A. Fitzgerald, *A Basic Life Spelling Vocabulary* (Milwaukee: Bruce Publishing Company, 1951).

[8] Ernest Horn, "Spelling," in *Encyclopedia of Educational Research,* Chester W. Harris, ed. (New York: The Macmillan Company, 3rd ed., 1960), p. 1346.

1. A preliminary term or monthly test to determine the general level of pupil spelling achievement.

2. A preliminary test on each lesson before instruction and study is begun on that lesson.

3. Study by each child of the words he misspelled on the pretest using a systematic or step-by-step study procedure.

4. One or more other tests on the lesson to indicate for each child the actual degree of his spelling mastery of the words involved.

5. The recording by each child of his test score and the listing of words to be reviewed.

6. The testing at regular intervals of the extent of mastery of review words.

How well children learn to spell depends primarily upon their attitudes toward spelling. Children who spell correctly in their written work outside of spelling class are those who are able to learn independently how to spell words they need to write and who have attitudes that show concern for making all spelling correct. Perhaps, then, the elementary teacher's main goal in spelling instruction should be to give pupils both a *consciousness* of correct spelling and a spelling *conscience*—a "kind of compulsion for correct written expression."[9] Attitudes may be improved by the teacher's following these practices:

1. Having the children study only those words which testing has shown them to be unable to spell. In the weekly lesson this is best done, as suggested previously by beginning the lesson with a pretest.

2. Providing the children with definite and efficient procedures for studying words rather than simply giving general instructions to study their spelling.

3. Regarding spelling as something that is important to good communication. This regard may be shown by the teacher's correct spelling, his use of the dictionary, and his insistence upon correct spelling of the words in the final products of children's written assignments.

4. Making children individually and as a class aware of their progress in learning spelling. This means the keeping of progress charts so that each child may know his and his class' achievement.

5. Teaching no more words in a given period than a child can successfully learn to spell. Repeated failures simply bring on more failures and feelings of resentment.

---

[9] E. L. Furness, "Psychological Determinants of Spelling Success," *Education, 79* (December, 1958), 237.

6. Making sure that the words the children are learning to spell are words that are important to them in their own writing. The children must also be aware of this importance; they may themselves examine writing samples and note the words that are used most frequently.

As suggested above a very important factor in the attainment of spelling goals is the procedure used in studying the spelling of a word. Most spelling authorities and authors of spelling textbooks are agreed that such procedure should involve visual, auditory, and kinesthetic approaches to the gaining of an image or impression of the word, interspersed with attempts to recall its spelling. The suggested procedure is usually to have the child:

1. Look at the word and pronounce it correctly.
2. Cover the word, pronounce it, and think how it looks.
3. Check himself and pronounce it again.
4. Cover the word and write it.
5. Check his spelling of it. If incorrect he must begin again at step one; if correct he may go on to the next word.

These steps may be modified for individual pupils. Some will be able to learn the spelling after following only the first two steps; others may need to say the word letter by letter or to follow the second and fourth steps more than once each time.

In addition to an established study procedure research bears out the importance of a number of other procedures which provide effective instructional programs. These include:

1. Presenting words to pupils for study in lists rather than in context. Presentation in context, while done to aid in developing meaning, is of little value if the words presented are those that the pupil needs in his writing and therefore already knows their meanings. Furthermore, contextual presentation is usually too brief to do more than use a word in a sentence, which may or may not really convey any meaning to it.

2. Using good test practices (see Chapter VI), including having each pupil correct his own tests so that his attention will focus upon his specific errors.

3. Spending no more than 60 to 75 minutes per week for spelling instruction. A spirited approach to the learning task will prevent dawdling and the development of poor listening and study habits, and will help build favorable attitudes toward correct spelling.

4. Learning no spelling rules that are not of practical value.[10] Helpful

---

[10] Ernest Horn, "Spelling," in *Encyclopedia of Educational Research*, p. 1345.

rules are those for dropping the final silent *e,* for changing *y* to *i,* for doubling the final consonant, for *u* following *q,* and those involving capitalization and punctuation. Time spent on the development of phonetic generalizations which are useful to reading but are of limited value to spelling can be more effectively spent in other ways. Such generalizations are best taught in connection with the problems children face in reading tasks.

5. Giving attention to the individual needs of pupils. The most practical way of doing this is to do some grouping for part of the instructional activities, to individualize words for study through use of the pretest, to provide individual help for pupils with special difficulties, and to expand the program for the more able spellers.

In helping the child who has spelling difficulty it is important to identify as accurately as possible the reasons for this difficulty and to be prompt in giving aid. Show him how to study a word; correct any bad habits of study he has; give him a chance to succeed by limiting his goals; and, above all, try to improve his reading skill.

The child who does well in spelling may be excused from all or most spelling instruction or he may be provided with activities which expand his vocabulary. Among the numerous worthwhile enrichment activities which may be provided are:

1. Finding synonyms and antonyms for words.
2. Using words in written sentences to show varied meanings.
3. Finding substitutes for overworked and dreary words.
4. Rewriting sentences to make them more appealing and convey meaning more effectively.
5. Defining words without the help of dictionaries and then checking these definitions.
6. Studying prefixes, suffixes, and root words, and building other words from these.
7. Searching out the history and origin of words.

Handwriting. The purpose of teaching handwriting in the schools is based upon its necessary role in communication. Handwriting is the principal tool of written expression. In order for such expression to be communicated adequately, the handwriting used must be legible. The school has the responsibility for teaching written expression; thus, it also has the responsibility for teaching children to write legibly. Observation in many classrooms would probably show conditions which seem to belie the fact that the school is assuming this responsibility. Children are apt to be sitting in all sorts of positions at their desks, with pencils or pens held in assorted ways, and with the papers upon which they are writing at angles which make legible writing difficult.

Teachers no longer stress the use of meaningless drill in the teaching of handwriting—nor should they. Neither do they advocate that all children attempt to learn one pattern or system of handwriting. They now are aware that some of their earlier emphasis on formal handwriting drill does not give proper recognition to the use of handwriting and to differences in development, skill, and ability in children. It is also true, however, that in too many instances their interest in recognizing differences and teaching for use has caused them to neglect principles of instruction in handwriting that are founded upon sound research evidence.

There is evidence, for example, to show that handwriting is made legible by (1) correct (common custom) letter formation, (2) uniform and adequate spacing between letters and between words, (3) uniform (for the individual) slant of all letters, (4) general alignment of letters, and (5) use of letters of appropriate size for the ability of the children, the distance between lines, the size of the paper, and the message written. There is evidence also that careful and neat arrangement of the writing adds to appearance and legibility.[11]

It is also necessary for the school to teach children to write with adequate speed for the tasks they have to do. This means that the writing must be done with ease in order for the attention of the writer to focus upon the words he is writing rather than upon the making of letters. Again, there is research showing that ease of writing is achieved through attention to (1) good posture, (2) correct pencil or pen holding, and (3) free and rhythmical arm and hand movement. Speed is also increased through conscious attempts to make strokes more rapidly and by decreasing the duration of pauses between strokes of the writing instrument.

As with the teaching of other skills, the teaching of handwriting is most effective when both the teacher and the children have attitudes which are favorable to its learning. Handwriting must be re-

---

[11] Recent summaries of research evidence concerning the teaching of handwriting include: Frank N. Freeman, *What Research Says to the Teacher: Teaching Handwriting* (Department of Classroom Teachers and the American Educational Research Association. Washington, D.C.: National Education Association, 1954); and Emma Myers, "A General Review of Handwriting Instruction." Unpublished Master's thesis, State University of Iowa, 1954.

garded as an important skill—one that is necessary for effective expression, and which must be learned. The teacher can help instill this attitude in the children by showing care in his own handwriting —by making certain that he forms letters correctly and neatly, by showing good posture as he writes, by writing smoothly and rhythmically, and by holding the pen, pencil, or chalk correctly. Children's attitudes toward handwriting will improve when they:

1. Write because there is a meaningful reason for writing.
2. Have considerable liberty in adjusting handwriting conditions to their own abilities and needs.
3. Are physically comfortable.
4. Have proper materials with which to write.
5. Experience thorough teaching of the handwriting skills.
6. Have ample opportunity to practice the skills they need to practice.
7. Are encouraged to evaluate their own handwriting in terms of the progress they are making.

Most schools teach manuscript (print-script) writing in the primary grades and make the transition to cursive writing in the early part of the third grade. The reasons for the rather general acceptance of teaching manuscript writing for the child's initial writing experiences are these:

1. It is easier to learn—only straight lines and simple curves are required.
2. It is typically more legible than cursive writing.
3. The form of the letters is similar to those which children encounter in reading.
4. Children derive great satisfaction because of the more rapid progress they are able to make.
5. Its use apparently contributes to achievement in reading, spelling, and the production of written expression.

Some schools continue instruction in manuscript along with the teaching of cursive after the initial transition is made. The ability is useful in making titles for charts and posters and in other lettering activities. A few schools do not teach cursive at all. Public pressure, however, including that of the children to do "real" writing, continues for teaching the cursive form; and the evidence at present does not support the claims that manuscript writing can be done as rapidly as can cursive writing.

Since studies have shown that manuscript writing seems to favor the development of fluency of written expression in the primary grades, there is currently a controversy concerning the most appropriate time for changing children from manuscript to cursive form. As was mentioned earlier, the majority of schools make the transition in the third grade. A few years ago the majority favored the latter half of the second grade. At present schools increasingly favor having the transition in the fourth grade. A satisfactory solution would appear to be varying the transition with different children. For most of them the point would seem to be near the end of the primarily oral program and the beginning of the more formal written program. Applying the programs advocated in this monograph, such time would be near the end of the second grade.

The teaching of left-handed children continues to be a problem, unwarranted though it may be. Hand dominance in children is usually fairly well-established by the time they are in school. Such dominance should not be changed. Sometimes, however, it is not easy to determine just what the dominance is. Such determination should not be left to casual observation; tests, such as throwing, putting pegs in holes, locking and unlocking a padlock, or cutting with scissors, should be used. If a child has a wavering or weak dominance, he should be encouraged to use his right hand for writing. If he shows definite left-hand dominance, the program should be adjusted to meet his needs.

The principal adjustment that needs to be made for left-handed children is the position of the paper. For right-handed children the paper should be tilted slightly to the left (perhaps 10 degrees) for manuscript and to about a 30-degree angle for cursive. For left-handed children the tilt of the paper should be to the opposite side. The purpose of placing the paper at the angles suggested is that the arm will always be approximately at a right angle to the lines of writing.

The actual procedures for teaching handwriting are usually adequately presented in the teacher's manuals that accompany the handwriting books children use. In addition, these suggestions may be useful:

1. Practice periods should be provided; practice during these periods should be upon individual needs.
2. Practice should be of short duration but should be frequent.

3. A checklist which keeps account of individual needs should be kept by the teacher.

4. Writing periods should follow periods of quiet activity rather than periods of strenuous movement.

5. Whenever possible practice should grow out of the needs shown in purposeful writing situations.

6. Children should learn to evaluate their own performance. Comparison may be made with levels of achievement shown on commercial scales as well as with their own previous writing efforts.

7. Samples of children's writing should be collected at intervals for analysis of their errors by the other pupils, the teacher, and other school authorities.

8. Constant attention to all details by teachers is necessary in order to establish good habits.

9. Too much stress on details by the teacher may be harmful; a better practice is to encourage the children in their evaluation.

10. Neatness in writing should be insisted upon—margins, indentations, centering of headings, erasures, and so forth.

Capitalization and punctuation. Capitalization and punctuation are mechanical elements of written language about which there is considerable evidence concerning needs of children at various grade levels. These mechanical elements also account for the major share of writing errors. Evidence of the importance of specific punctuation and capitalization items, and the frequency of error in their use, has been rather firmly established through examination of the directed and spontaneous writing of children and adults. Therefore, curriculum guides and textbooks in language may be quite precise in their listings of grade-level requirements. It is well to remember, however, that within a given classroom there will be considerable variation in abilities to use specific items correctly, as well as some variation in the needs for them. Furthermore, there is some tendency to list a far greater number of items than studies have shown to be important.

The following grade-level listing of capitalization skills may be an adequate guide to a teacher's analysis of class needs. Essentially it is a minimal and suggestive listing only; it does, however, give attention to the needs of children and to the relative difficulty of the items:

GRADE ONE

a. The first word in a sentence.
b. The child's name.

c. The pronoun *I*.

d. The names of his teacher, school, town, etc.

GRADE TWO

a. Names of days and months.

b. Names of titles: *Mr., Mrs., Miss.*

c. Proper names used in daily writing.

d. First and important words in titles of books and stories.

GRADE THREE

a. First word in a line of verse.

b. First word of salutation, as "Dear," and of closing, as "Yours."

c. Names of holidays.

GRADE FOUR

a. Names of cities and states and other geographical names.

b. "Mother" and "Father" when used in place of the name.

c. Names of organizations, as *Boy Scouts, Grade Four,* and so forth.

GRADE FIVE

a. Names of all places and persons, countries, oceans, and so forth.

b. Capitalization necessary in outlining.

c. Titles when used with names, such as *President Lincoln.*

d. Commercial trade names.

GRADE SIX

a. First word of a quoted sentence.

b. Proper adjectives, showing race, nationality, and so forth.

c. The Bible and names for the Deity.

d. Abbreviations of proper nouns and titles.

Minimal punctuation items, and their suggested grade for instructional introduction are:

GRADE ONE

a. Period at the end of a declarative sentence.

b. Period after the numerals in a listing.

GRADE TWO

a. Question mark at the end of a question.

b. Comma after the salutation in a friendly letter.

c. Comma after the closing in a friendly letter.

d. Comma between the day of the month and the year in the writing of a date.

e. Comma between the name of a city and the name of a state when written together.

GRADE THREE

a. Period after an abbreviation or initial.
b. Apostrophe in common contractions, such as *isn't, aren't, I'll.*
c. Commas between words in a list.

GRADE FOUR

a. Apostrophe in words to show possession.
b. Exclamation point at the end of an exclamatory statement.
c. Period following a command.
d. Commas setting off appositives.
e. Colon after the salutation of a business letter.
f. Quotation marks around direct quotations.
g. Comma between explanatory words and a quotation.
h. Periods after numbers or letters in an outline.
i. Hyphen showing division of a word at the end of a line.

GRADE FIVE

a. Colon in writing time, as *8:40.*
b. Comma to show changed word order.
c. Underlining the title of a book.
d. Quotation marks around the titles of booklets, pamphlets, poems, stories, and the name of a chapter in a book.

GRADE SIX

a. Commas setting off nouns in direct address.
b. Colon at the beginning of a list.
c. Hyphen in compound numbers.
d. Commas in sentences as needed to make meaning clear.

As these lists of punctuation and capitalization items suggest, children tend to have need for virtually the same elements at every grade level. Teachers generally will know, and studies have borne out, that little improvement is made in ability to use these elements as the grade level advances. The use, lack of use, or misuse of punctuation and capitalization skills becomes habitual. The continuance of errors in using these skills indicates teaching program deficiencies in (1) motivating learning, (2) practicing the skills before they have been adequately taught, and/or (3) not insisting upon the correct use of a particular item or items after they have been taught and practiced.

Basic principles which should be followed in instruction are:

1. Emphasizing few items—only those for which there is genuine need.

2. Creating realistic situations which demand use of these items.

3. Making a clear impression as to what is correct by using a model, by discussing the problem, by showing examples of the correct and incorrect, and by practicing specifically upon the item.

4. Insisting upon the correct use of the item after it has been introduced and a clear impression made.

The following teaching suggestions amplify the principles and may prove useful in developing increasingly greater punctuation and capitalization skill:

1. Begin instruction by giving simple diagnostic tests which focus upon the use or misuse of specific capitalization or punctuation items and, thus, identify areas and items for instructional emphasis.

2. Keep simple records of errors made in daily work. This calls for careful observation and is useful in further determining instructional needs.

3. Give exercises which require children to verify the uses of capital letters or other punctuation items. The object of this is to acquaint children with irregularities in general practice and among sources commonly used as standards.

4. Use dictation drills which require the practice of punctuation and capitalization knowledge; both sentences and paragraphs may be dictated. This type of exercise is also good for teaching "sentence sense." The exercises should be directed as much as possible to the needs of each child.

5. Have the children check their own writing after the dictation exercises. All instruction should emphasize self-diagnosis of difficulties.

6. Provide proofreading drills which emphasize the punctuation and capitalization items with which a pupil has difficulty.

7. Make frequent further use of short diagnostic tests on the capitalization and punctuation items that are of major importance, or which are causing the most difficulty. Again, each child should check his own work.

8. Insist that each pupil critically edit and proofread whatever he writes.

9. Make all drill and practice periods short and related to specific needs. Frequent five-minute drills are much better than less frequent drills of longer duration.

10. Emphasize the importance of proper punctuation to good sentence structure and conveying meaning. Present examples of this whenever possible.

11. Encourage the careful use of capitals and punctuation in all the

pupils' work. Stress continually the importance of good form as an aid to effective writing.

Proofreading. The development of ability in and the habit of proofreading to find and correct the child's own errors in written expression should be an important part of the language instructional program. Children may recognize the need for writing in a particular situation; they may make use of a model in their writing; they may formulate standards for the writing; they may give attention to possible errors in usage, spelling, and punctuation; and they may give attention to the content of what they write, although through all of this they may not have reread what they wrote nor given any thoughtful consideration to making improvement after it is once written.

To do effective proofreading, a child must have definite initial instruction and continuing guided encouragement and insistence upon using the proofreading skills he has learned. The first-grade teacher will encourage the children to read carefully what has been written as a group composition. Attention will be called to examining each sentence to see if it begins with a capital letter, if it ends with a period or question mark if that is needed, and if the words really say what was intended. Such first-grade instruction will lead to later attention to these details in what the pupil writes for himself. In early stages of instruction, also, the teacher may make use of samples that are written on the chalkboard for consideration by the entire class. Occasionally this sample may be one of the children's. Children may also occasionally proofread each other's work as practice, while keeping in mind that proofreading is a personal habit.

In addition, teachers will find it helpful to have the children develop proofreading criteria by which expressional activities may be examined. At first these criteria should be limited to only one or two details. Later they may be expanded to include further items of organization, form, and mechanics. Sometimes the criteria may relate to both mechanics and content; at other times the criteria may relate to only one. For example, criteria dealing only with content might state:

1. Is my story told in good order?
2. Does each paragraph tell about one topic?
3. Is each sentence in a paragraph about the topic?

4. Are there any words I should change because they are uninteresting or don't say what I mean?

5. Is each sentence a good sentence?

It is also a useful technique to have children read their written work aloud in order to help them locate usage errors and incorrect or omitted punctuation.

Using sources of information. The development of the skills needed for efficient and effective use of printed sources of information is of major inportance to both written and oral expression. These skills and their teaching are discussed in this chapter since generally their use calls for writing, even though the final expressional product may be oral.

The dictionary. Dictionary skills are often taught in connection with the reading program or the spelling program. A systematic approach in either of these areas or in a separate program in which the specific skills are taught is essential, while use should be made of the skills in any activity in which there is a need.

Dictionary skills to be taught in the primary grades include learning the names of letters, learning to recognize each one, and learning alphabetical order. In the middle and upper grades further and more specific dictionary skills must be taught, as suggested by this listing of dictionary activities:[12]

1. Alphabetizing lists of words beginning with different letters.

2. Alphabetizing lists of words beginning with the same letter.

3. Alphabetizing lists of words beginning with two or more of the same letters, such as pantaloon, pancake, panacea, panic, panther, and pancreas.

4. Developing speed and accuracy in using the guide words at the top of each page.

5. Understanding the diacritical markings used in the dictionary.

6. Using the pronunciation key, accented syllables, and other aids to correct pronunciation.

7. Noting stems and affixes.

8. Selecting the best of alternative meanings.

9. Making use of homonyms, synonyms, and antonyms.

10. Knowing special parts of the dictionary, such as lists of abbreviations and the biographical dictionary.

---

[12] David H. Russell, *Children Learn to Read* (Boston: Ginn & Company, 2nd ed., 1961), p. 290.

Indexes, tables of contents, and glossaries. The skills needed to make use of these sections of books must also receive instructional attention in the elementary school. The best time for beginning instruction in any of these areas is when a book with an index, table of contents, or glossary is first used. Attention in the teaching should be upon their practical help in locating information. In each of these sections of books rather specific skills and information must be taught. For example, in using an index a child would need to know:

1. The difference between topics and sub-topics.
2. What the different punctuation marks in the index mean.
3. How maps, graphs, tables, or diagrams are shown in an index.
4. The use and significance of the key or directions at the beginning or the end of the index.
5. Different types of arrangement of sub-topics.
6. How the pages of the most important discussions on the particular topic are shown.
7. Whether or not pronunciation is indicated in an index.
8. Knowledge that it may be necessary to look under more than one topic before finding the information wanted.

Other reference sources. Children also need to learn the use of the encyclopedia, almanac, atlas, reader's guides, and card files. The use of some of these is taught, of course, in high schools; but if children are going to develop skill in their use, introductory teaching must begin in the elementary grades. Introducing reader's guides, card catalogs, and other library aids in high school is in many instances too late to develop in children a genuine appreciation of and interest in libraries and the ideas and facts that may be found in books. Attempting to teach library skills in the absence of an adequate library is useless, however, and would better be omitted until the child actually has such a library to use.

The use of encyclopedias begins in many schools almost as soon as the children have developed some facility in reading. Items should be taught systematically, and should be reviewed as often as there is indication of the pupils' inefficient use or a general lack of use of encyclopedias. Specific items to be taught should include the following:

1. Knowledge as to how material is arranged in a particular encyclopedia, and how it might be arranged in others.
2. An understanding of the use of the index in an encyclopedia.

3. An understanding of the meaning of guide words and letters on the covers of volumes.

4. Skill in skimming a page to locate specific information.

5. Skill in using cross references, guide words, pronunciation keys, and topic headings.

A good practice for the teaching of reference skills and for maintaining these skills is the provision of specific exercises. For example, children might be instructed to answer such questions as:

1. What book and what page in the encyclopedia tells about coal?

2. What will be on the first line of an author card in the card catalog?

3. Who is the author of *Children in Other Lands?*

4. Where would you look to find the origin of the word *belfry?*

5. What is the call number of the book *Little Women?*

CHAPTER V

Improving Usage and Composition

The quality of usage and composition is of basic importance to the effectiveness of both oral and written expression. This fact would undoubtedly be readily conceded by all; and while concern with matters of usage and composition has been a focal point in discussions of effective communication in the preceding chapters, the emphasis has been on the pupils' learning to express themselves with ease and effectiveness in situations which are natural and purposeful. The importance of usage and composition and the need for giving specific attention to developing habits and skills in these areas—particularly since the grammatical approach to teaching usage and composition is stressed by some teachers—suggests the need for a more detailed consideration of them here. Attention will be directed first to improving usage and later to compositional factors.

A Functional Approach to Grammar and Usage Teaching

The teaching of grammar in schools continues to be the subject of controversy even after fifty years of accumulated research evidence. Most authorities today concede that teaching formal grammar as the basis for the improvement of expression has failed. Many different beliefs exist, however, concerning a more functional approach to teaching the things formal grammar was supposed to teach, the value, if any, of grammatical knowledge, and the definitions given to various elements of composition and expression. Further, many differences exist not only among teachers but among others in our society as to the acceptability or "correctness" of many words and expressions.

Relationship of grammar and usage. The terms *grammar* and *usage* are often confused. Grammar, to some persons, refers to the kind of knowledge and discipline that supposedly is the basis for "correct" language expression. To others, grammar is used to describe all the elements involved in oral and written composition, including the mechanical ones of punctuation and capitalization. To add to the confusion, "grammar" is variously defined in dictionaries, with at least one unabridged dictionary giving seven different meanings for the term.

Perhaps the clearest statement as to the distinction between grammar and usage has been made by Nemec and Pooley.[1] They suggested that the term *grammar* be used to apply to the systematic study of the structure of the language and that matters of actual language use be called *usage*. No distinction is to be made concerning the "correctness" or "incorrectness" of usage—only the "acceptability" or "unacceptability" of it in a particular situation. Of course, the teaching of usage which is acceptable in cultured circles of society is the ultimate goal of the school's program, but, even so, our language is regarded as alive, growing, and changing, a language whose acceptability is not derived from any historical ground or logical principle. A particular usage may gain acceptance as good usage; its function may then be described using the terminology of grammar. Grammar, then, is not regarded as something final and static, but as an organized means of describing the accepted usage habits of educated persons. If these habits change, the grammatical definition changes.

The role of grammar in an instructional program. All of the arguments which have arisen from the lack of a common understanding of terminology have resulted in many differences over the function of grammar in the teaching of language expression. Defenders of the belief that grammar is a set of laws and rules to which usage must conform have rushed to the defense of rules, classifications, parsing, and diagramming as being essential to the creation of expression and the understanding of that which is received. On the other hand, others have determined that the failure of grammar to succeed as a method for improving expression means that all attempts to improve usage and matters of form should be abandoned. Neither of these conclusions is justified. Failure to recognize both that as language habits change and that

---

[1] Lois G. Nemec and Robert C. Pooley, "Children's Experiences with Usage and Functional Grammar," in *Children and the Language Arts,* ed. by Virgil E. Herrick and Leland B. Jacobs (Englewood Cliffs: Prentice-Hall, Inc., 1955), p. 289.

pupils learn to do what they habitually practice results in an inadequate instructional program.

The recognition of the changing nature of language has led to interest in new grammatical terminology derived from linguistic studies. Many high schools are experimenting with the teaching of "linguistics," "structural linguistics," "transitional grammar," and so on, with many of the experiments calling for the learning of new grammatical terminology. To what extent these experiments will spread to the elementary schools is not now known. Present evidence indicates, however, that the experiments give the high school students better appreciation of language but, as has been the case with the teaching of formal conventional grammar, with little effect upon their competency in speaking and writing.

It is well to remember that the elementary school language program has as its major goals the development of effective expression in the many situations calling for use of language in which children and adults engage and the development of attitudes, skills, and abilities which contribute to this expressional efficiency. The place of grammar in a program with such objectives is determined by the contribution it makes to their attainment. The inclusion of grammar teaching as the basis for the elimination of undesirable usage is not defensible. However, in the process of constructing sentences and paragraphs children must manipulate various sentence elements. Such manipulation will lead to the gaining of concepts concerning those elements. Manipulation will begin, of course, in the primary grades and will focus upon constructing sentences which make sense. In the upper grades, appropriate grammatical terminology may be applied to the words in a sentence and to parts of the sentence in relation to each other. This learning of grammar occurs as a need emerges; the emphasis is always upon the production of effective expression for the specific occasion.

The objectives of a functional grammar program suggested in *An Experience Curriculum in English,* a publication of the National Council of Teachers of English, a number of years ago are worthy objectives today.[2] These are:

---

[2] *An Experience Curriculum in English,* A Report of the Curriculum Commission of the National Council of Teachers of English, W. Wilbur Harfield, Chairman (New York: Appleton-Century-Crofts, Inc., 1935), pp. 230–33.

1. To reduce the tendency to speak and especially to write fragmentary sentences by acquiring the concept of the sentence as a group of words which makes sense.

2. To guard further against fragmentary sentences by extending the concept of the sentence.

3. To reduce the tendency to speak and especially to write run-on sentences, whether with or without *and,* by sharpening the concept of the sentence as the expression of a single thought.

4. To provide variety in sentences by learning to shift adverbs and adverbial phrases.

5. To secure speed and ease in narrative by combining sentences with the same subjects into sentences with compound predicates.

6. To secure sentence variety and paragraph coherence by learning to use initial adverbial clauses, especially those introduced by *when* and *if*.

7. To increase effectiveness and accuracy of expression by learning to use adverbial clauses in the predicate position.

8. To increase vividness and color of statements by means of adverbs (modifiers of verbs) in the predicate position.

9. To increase vividness and color by increased and more accurate use of modifying adjectives.

10. To improve ease and clarity of statement by employing simple relative clauses (with the relative as subject).

This functional approach to attaining and using grammatical knowledge begins with the writing and speaking of sentences and stresses saying a thing clearly, completely, and interestingly, rather than beginning with the study of subjects and predicates or nouns and verbs. As a child writes, he gradually learns the concept of proper and common nouns, the limiting and descriptive effects of some words upon others, and that sometimes words tell *how, when,* or *where.* He begins to realize that in order for a sentence to be clear it must have two parts: one tells who or what is the doer; the other expresses what is being done. As such realization takes place the terms *subject* and *predicate* may be introduced and talked about. Later, *noun, pronoun,* and *verb* are introduced in the same manner; the same may be done for *adverb* and *adjective.* Still later reference may be made to *clauses* and *phrases.* Understanding of the various concepts is gradual and the naming of them is not done until such understanding is functioning.

The functional approach to teaching grammatical elements useful for improving communication is not unplanned, nor dependent upon incidental occurrences. Careful planning of opportunities for motivated teaching and learning is basic. At each grade level the teacher should take advantage of the naturally occurring language situations to plan for the inclusion of grammatical understandings helpful to clear presentation of thought. Usually the elements of grammar which are needed in the formulation of children's expression arise naturally when an active language program is in effect; elements which do not so occur are probably not of sufficient importance to justify their being taught.

English language usage. Patterns of usage occurring in the speech and writing of children often persist year after year in spite of teachers' efforts to bring about changes. Many reasons for this have been advanced; among them are:

1. The degree of firmness in which the habits a child brings to school have been fixed.
2. The continuance of the same environmental forces upon language habits during out-of-school hours.
3. The disinterest of the child in changing usage habits which would set him off from his normal environment.
4. The all too often inadequate language program of the school with respect to providing situations for real exercise of correct language habits.
5. The use of ineffectively motivated and taught lessons on usage.

These reasons lend support to the principle long advocated in language instruction that the number of usage items for teaching in the elementary grades should be quite limited. Supporting this principle, too, it has been suggested that ninety per cent of usage problems in the elementary grades consist of the repetition of a rather small number of errors, and that many so-called errors are not errors at all but are appropriate language for children of these ages. The following sections suggest usage elements which should properly receive some instructional emphasis in the elementary school program.

Verb forms. Studies have long shown that a high percentage of all usage errors are made in the forms of some of the most commonly used verbs. Not all errors in verb usage need instructional emphasis in the elementary school; many errors are of an individual nature and a child should be encouraged to eliminate these as a personal matter. However, a limited number of errors are of general concern and should receive the principal instructional emphasis. Usually these include:[3]

1. Errors in tense, such as *says* for *said, come* for *came, run* for *ran,* have *did* for have *done, give* for *gave, ask* for *asked,* has *took* for has *taken.*

2. Using the wrong verb, as *learn* for *teach, guess* for *think, set* for *sit, leave* for *let.*

3. Lack of agreement with subject in number, as *we was* for *we were; girls helps* for *girls help; you was* for *you were; Bill and Mary is going* for *Bill and Mary are going.*

4. Illiteracies, such as *knowed, git, et, ain't, throwed.*

Pronouns. Not much difficulty is encountered by children in learning that a pronoun is a convenient substitute for a noun. Further, children can readily see that often the effectiveness of expression may be increased by such substitution. In spite of the ease with which these concepts are learned, many errors occur in the selection of pronouns. Some of these errors are:

1. Use as subject but not in nominative case, as *Me and my father went to town.*

2. Use as object of a verb or preposition but not in the objective case, as *Father sent Bill and I.*

3. *Who* for persons, *which* for all other objects.

4. Illiteracies, such as *youse, yourn, hisen, hern.*

5. Incorrect formation of compound pronouns, such as *hisself, theirselves.*

6. Indefinite references, as *It was lying on the porch* or *Alice told her Mother that she was wrong.*

Antecedents. Lack of clarity in expression often results from using a pronoun which doesn't agree with the noun or noun equivalent to which it refers. This type of error is frequent in the speech and writing of young children; however, a teacher should not become so concerned with the following of rules relating to agreement of pronoun and antecedent that expressions acceptable in present-day standard usage are regarded as errors. For example, although such sentences as *Everybody get in their seats* and *Everyone said that they were going* technically violate the agreement rule, the meaning in each case is clear and the usage is

---

[3] A most useful listing is given in Robert C. Pooley, *Teaching English Usage* (New York: Appleton-Century-Crofts, Inc., 1946), pp. 179–80.

rather generally accepted, particularly in speaking. Regardless of this, however, the principle of correcting first the worst errors in lack of agreement should be followed, and it is not likely that either of these examples need be attacked in the elementary school. The worst errors occur in expressions in which there is no consistency of number in the expression or in which the pronoun does not clearly refer to its antecedent.

Redundancy. Errors of redundancy occur frequently and present difficulties to teachers in their elimination. Among the most common are: *John he, this here, that there,* and *Where is it at?*

Double negatives. Errors in the use of double negatives are not too frequent; but, when found, their use is generally rather firmly established. The most common are *haven't no* and *don't know nothing.*

Miscellaneous errors. In addition to those above, the following types occur often enough that their correction is generally necessary: (1) The use of needless introductory words, as *then, well, so, listen, why, say.* (2) The needless repetition of words, as *That's what he said. He said that.* (3) Confusion of words, as *it's* for *its.*

Teaching language usage. The use of good English depends almost entirely upon a foundation of habitual use of acceptable expression—habits so firmly founded as to be automatic. Only in very formal language situations does a proficient adult speaker or writer become conscious of the need for close discrimination in language choices. Even then, his language habits are the principal bases for selecting the particular words and choosing the appropriate usages. The almost ineradicable nature of firmly fixed habits and the place of habit formation in learning language have been discussed earlier in this monograph. These facts on learning are of no greater importance in any area of language instruction than they are in the teaching of correct usage. The basic psychological principle that is the core of instruction in effective expression is that habits are developed and made automatic through the repeated exercise of responses under motivating conditions which favor those responses. In expression the response might be either a substandard usage or an acceptable one; in either case the extent to which the usage becomes a habit is dependent upon the motivating conditions.

Little good will result from teaching efforts unless pupils want to improve their usage. Each child must be made to feel that improving his usage will be of personal benefit to him. He must be convinced that his communication will be more effective in situations and with people important to him if he is to be successful in changing a particular usage habit. The only exception to this motivational approach occurs usually in the primary grades—but sometimes later—where the immaturity of the child may cause him to be unaware of the need to change a habit. In those circumstances, major dependence should be placed upon continuous incidental correction of poor usages by the substitution of the acceptable forms and by adequate provision of situations where there is opportunity for practice because of a genuine need for speaking and writing.

Good usage habits are best established in a classroom where the child is motivated by pleasant conditions and a clear understanding of the purposes for an expressional activity. Particular attention must also be given to the use of oral drill rather than written drill. The importance of sound in teaching usage has repeatedly been emphasized in educational literature, yet continued emphasis tends to be placed upon written exercises.[4] Since there is a general tendency to write as we talk rather than to talk as we write, most usage practice must be heard and spoken to be effective. Such practice must occur in settings of normal and natural use of language and for purposes which are genuine and recognized as such by pupils.

It is imperative that the exact usage errors a child makes be identified before practice begins. This means carefully cataloging each pupil's errors for individual attention and for selecting the most frequently occurring and serious errors for class attack. Every teacher should keep a file of cards or a checklist for jotting down the usage errors made by children. Corrective instruction should begin as soon as errors are noted; such instruction must be adequately motivated; the incorrect and correct usages must be seen, heard, and said by the pupil; practice must be provided in the correct usage; the correct form must be put into practical use with no intervening use of the incorrect form allowed.

No drill materials should be used until a child is properly motivated and until he adequately understands both the incorrect

---

[4] See, for example, *Teaching Language in the Elementary School*, Forty-third Yearbook of the National Society for the Study of Education, Part II (Chicago: University of Chicago Press, 1944).

and the correct usage. One reason that written practice materials have produced less than the desired results in establishing good usage is that too often these materials have been used before the child has been ready for the practice. The effectiveness of practice or drill materials in establishing good usage may be improved through observance of these suggestions:

1. Conducting lively oral drills for five or ten minutes a day.
2. Basing drill upon what has been found during that day to be needed.
3. Varying the time of day for the drills.
4. Creating some individualization in the drill by placing children making the same types of errors in special groups.
5. Individualizing written drill by securing two or more copies of each of several language workbooks for the grade. Cut each book into separate sheets and mount these on stiff paper; do the same for material secured from other sources and mimeographed or duplicated. Arrange materials alphabetically according to type of error. These materials may be used in conjunction with inventory sheets of errors that the children make.
6. Have pupils keep notebooks of their own most persistent usage errors.
7. Make certain that there is understanding of the purposes of any drill; also, make clear any explanatory material that is a part of the drill activities.

Developing the Rhetorical Skills

The rhetorical skills are those dealing with sentence construction: how sentences are made clear, concise, and interesting; and how sentences are organized into paragraphs or larger units of expression. This section suggests procedures for helping pupils construct good sentences, adding variety and interest to those sentences, organizing facts and ideas, and selecting and enriching the vocabulary they use in expression.

Sentence structure. The development of ability in the construction of good sentences in both oral and written expression is a basic teaching problem at every grade level. In too many cases, improper instruction is offered because teachers have given inadequate thought to precisely what is involved in the instruction. Good sentences are possible only as the constructor of the sentence is thinking clearly. An awkward or poorly constructed sentence, or an expression that is less than a sentence, is usually the result of a struggle to describe an idea or feeling that has been poorly thought out. The realization that clear thinking is the basic ingredient of good sentences should give a teacher a precise direction to follow in teaching effective sentence construction.

Children who have ample opportunity for expression for actual purposes, and who are guided in making such expression as effective as possible, will develop abilities in clear thinking. With the focus upon genuine communication, children will give thought to what is to be said and how best to say it. Every expression a child makes in a well-planned language program must receive the conscious effort of both himself and his teacher toward making that expression intelligible. This effort must be constant and continuing; there are no shortcuts. The kindergarten teacher must begin the program by giving pupils many opportunities for talking, by helping them to speak of one thing at a time, and by making reference to individual sentences:

> "Listen to my next *sentence*."
> "Tell me in one *sentence* what we do at the beginning of story time."
> "Think what was the most interesting thing we saw on our trip yesterday. You tell me, John, and I will write your *sentence*."

Teachers should be cautious about defining a sentence as a group of words expressing a whole or complete thought. Actually there is little instructional need for a definition. Instead of attempting a definition, a sentence should be thought of as a device for expressing an idea. Attention should thus be given to the idea and the expression of that idea in a way that is clear and exact. With continual emphasis upon clarity, upon the statement of the thought, children will gain the concept of the sentence. They will discover that a sentence always has two parts, subject and predicate, either expressed or implied. They will discover that a sentence states something; that sometimes other elements are needed to give the sentence clarity, exactness, and interest. In short, they will gain "sentence sense."

The major faults in sentence construction are those in which the thought is unclear and vague because something is missing or in which the thought is lost due to rambling and the inclusion of too many words and ideas. The first of these faults may be caused by the children's thinking getting ahead of their writing or speaking, so that some words or ideas are simply omitted. A fragmented sentence also may result from an inadequate understanding of the subject-predicate concept; thus, either the subject or predicate, or elements of them, are not expressed, nor are they clearly implied. The latter type of construction error occurs as more or less complete and separate ideas are joined by *and* or *but,* and as rambling, and again more or less complete, statements are either unseparated or are incorrectly separated by punctuation and capitalization.

The correction of any of these faults is dependent upon the same instructional approach as that suggested above for teaching sentence sense. Each of the faults is a result of inadequate understanding and sensitiveness to the concept of a sentence. For children to attain this understanding, a systematic instructional program should be used throughout a school at every grade level.

Variety and interest. Interest must be present in an expression for communication to take place. The speaker or writer whose expression is monotonous in form and without words or ideas to arouse his audience is not really communicating. Of course, much commonplace and dull expression does occur and may very well be perfectly "correct" structurally and mechanically, but this is not the type of expression the language teacher should be trying to teach. It may be, too, that a reader or listener will get limited meaning from such expression, but it is unlikely that attention will be maintained without factors of interest being present.

The content of expression may of itself be of interest to an audience, and certainly attention should be given first to the selection of content which will be of interest to those to whom it is directed. But there are other ways to arouse interest or to add to the interest in the content. Of course, the clarity of the expression, the understanding a reader or a listener may get from it, should not be sacrificed in striving for interest. The use of illustrative stories and anecdotes within the expression, the use of colorful and forceful words, the use of action and action words, the use of words that create moods and cause feelings, and the exclusion of superfluous details should all add to understanding as well as create interest.

Interest may also be added through variety in the order of words and grammatical elements within a sentence. In spite of a tendency to make them so, sentences do not always have to be in subject-verb-object order. Children should learn this and recognize that beginning with a modifying clause or phrase may add to both interest and clarity. They should also understand that the misplacement of a modifier or of an antecedent may cause confusion and create disinterest.

Children may be shown the importance of interest factors by having them select stories which have appealed to them and then tell why they have been interesting. General answers that they give may be pursued by the teacher and class until specific factors such as colorful phrases, appealing characterization, or surprise climaxes are identified. With recognition of the importance of interest factors, children may practice changing their sentences and paragraphs so that they are more interesting. They may also try to say things in different ways as practice in varying word order.

Organization. The importance of organization to effective expression was stressed in Chapter IV in the discussion of outlining. As was suggested there, organization begins as a child first sees relationships. This should be in the kindergarten and the teacher takes advantage of it, encouraging children to classify and to put things that go together in lists. Many activities found later in reading class, and such things as telling a story in proper sequence, putting together a puzzle, and listing steps to follow in a game are all organizational activities. Problems of organization of expression are really problems in thinking. Organizing is a thinking process. If information or an idea is to be expressed in a clearly organized fashion, it first must be clearly understood by the person making the expression. The development of a child's ability to organize his thinking must precede his becoming skilled in arranging the order of his facts in written or spoken expression.

Organization of thought in expression involves (1) sticking to the subject, (2) relating information in some systematic and effective sequence, (3) limiting ideas or information to the solution of a problem or some other specific purpose, and (4) basing interpretation and generalization upon fact and experience. These are involved whether the expression is a sentence or a larger unit of expression. Suggestions for the teaching of organizational skills are included in the following sections dealing with the sentence and the paragraph.

Order of ideas within the sentence. There is no set formula for the presentation of ideas within a sentence. Most commonly the subject is first and is followed by the predicate. The overuse of this form has led to many dull and uninteresting sentences being written and spoken. Actually, almost any word or phrase may be used to begin a sentence or to end it so long as the sentence makes sense and clearly and fully explains the intended ideas as effectively as would some other arrangement of words. Children may improve their simple sentences and learn to use increasingly the compound and compound-complex sentences through a language program calling for much purposeful speaking and writing. Occasionally, as a child uses a simple sentence, he may be encouraged to transpose an appositive to the beginning position, to place a word or phrase modifier at the beginning, to eliminate unnecessary words, or to add modifiers which add to the accuracy of the expression. This procedure should be informal and should focus upon making sentences more interesting, varied, and meaningful. As children become more fluent, further suggestions for using other sentence patterns may be made.

The run-on sentence is a problem at most grade levels and is due to the difficulty children have in keeping ideas distinct and to the unsureness they feel about punctuation usages. The most common connective used in running simple sentences together is *and,* with *but* also being used frequently. Children need to learn that using compound sentences—sentences requiring the use of connectives —is one way to provide interest and variety of expression but that their use may be overdone. Suggestions for teaching the proper use of connectives include:

1. Write on the board a paragraph which has short choppy sentences. Have the children decide which sentences should be combined and how to combine them.

2. Write several compound sentences on the board and have the children find the connectives.

3. Have the children bring to class sentences from their writing which show how they used connectives properly.

4. Discuss with the class the relationship of the two major parts of a sentence such as "Mary was tired, and she began to cry." Lead the class

to select some other word as a substitute for *and* and, later, do a complete reorganization of the sentence.

5. Keep a list of connectives, such as:

and	since	wherever	before
so	until	whenever	as soon as
but	where	that	then
if	when	because	after
who	which	although	unless

6. Continually show children how particular connectives are used. They should discover that:

and is used to join ideas of equal importance.

so, therefore, since, because show cause or reason.

when indicates time.

whenever indicates time and repetition.

but is used when there is something unexpected to follow.

who, which, that are good substitutes for *and, he,* and *it.*

Order of sentences within the paragraph. The idea of the paragraph may be taught in the primary grades as children learn to write single sentences and, later, paragraphs of two or three sentences. The emphasis in this beginning instruction is that a new idea being introduced or unrelated information being added requires a new paragraph. This approach stresses the point that a paragraph has a main idea and that everything in it relates to this idea. Points to remember in teaching paragraph organization and suggested procedures include the following:

1. Show children how proper use of paragraphs and good organization within a paragraph aids clarity of expression. This may be done principally by use of samples of their own writing.

2. Regularly inspect children's writing for sentence sequence and make suggestions for improvement.

3. Encourage children to watch for ways in which professional writers move skillfully from topic to topic and use paragraphs in their writing.

4. Demonstrate the importance of the beginning and ending sentences in paragraphs.

5. Use exercises such as those which call for determining where one paragraph ends and another begins in writing that has been deliberately run together.

Vocabulary. The best way to give breadth and depth to children's vocabularies is to provide many opportunities for interesting and challenging experiences. This may be done in many ways and in all areas of the curriculum, but such provision must be supplemented by conscious attention to the meanings of new words and new concepts encountered in the experiences. Helpful for the development of word meaning and use are the following:

1. Listing on the board new words encountered in classroom activities, or brought to class by children from their reading and other experiences at home. Discussion of these words is necessary and perhaps the writing of the meanings will be helpful.

2. Having the children keep a listing of their individual new words in notebooks. This should not be made a tiresome task, such as having a requirement of a minimum number of words daily, but should be made something they are actually interested in doing.

3. Making of charts listing "quiet" words, or perhaps "sound," "gay," or "sad" words. There are many ways these may be expanded. For example, words for special occasions may be listed. Such occasions might be Christmas, a campfire, a boat trip, or a horseback ride.

4. Noticing alliteration and rhyme in slogans and posters, picturesque and descriptive phrases, mood words, and interesting word derivatives.

5. Suggesting interesting topics and ideas for oral or written composition. Topics such as the following will bring forth many new words as well as words that are not used as frequently as they should be.

1. The Feel of Autumn.
2. How Our Backyard Looks Today.
3. Above the Timber Line.
4. Sounds Along the Lakeshore.
5. The Life of a Blade of Grass.

The best experience children can have, of course, for the building of vocabulary is extensive reading. For some children this avenue may be partly closed because of limitations in their reading skill. The close relationship between vocabulary development and reading skill is clearly present. Reading is limited by vocabulary development and vocabulary development is limited by reading deficiency. The development of the two must go along together.

CHAPTER VI

Evaluating Language Expression

In too many instances the relationship of objectives and instructional procedures in language to evaluation is treated superficially or not at all. The authors of a number of language arts methods textbooks, as well as other writers in current periodical literature, often leave the reader with the impression that any attempt at evaluation of language products and skills other than a subjective and cursory appraisal by the teacher is not only futile but runs counter to the best interests of the school, the teacher, and the pupil. This seems to be an opinion held in spite of the rather firm establishment of the principle that evaluation is an essential component of effective teaching. This ignoring of the need to determine accomplishment, to diagnose the product of individual effort, and to base judgments upon such measurements may be accounted for by the individuals' unfortunate experiences with measuring instruments. It is true that the complex nature of the expressional skills has placed limitations upon the production of valid and reliable measuring instruments. This fact, combined with the placement of undue reliance upon some measuring instruments, possibly led to the unfortunate experiences. Undoubtedly such experiences to some extent have led also to the current emphasis in evaluation upon using less precise and objective measuring instruments than the testing instruments which have been generally considered to be the bases for evaluation. Attention to the development and use of instruments other than the familiar tests is justified in programs of evaluation. However, this does not mean that evaluation does not need to be as precise and objective as possible; nor does it mean that measurement is not necessary before evaluative judgments are made.

The importance of careful evaluation in an instructional program is indicated by an examination of the following steps in a typical program:

1. Administering inventory tests or other instruments which attempt to determine, preceding the teaching, the learning achievements of the individuals comprising the class. Such instruments should confront the pupils with situations calling for responses to the precise abilities or skills included in the instructional program. This approach prevents the learner's wasting time studying facts or skills he has already mastered, and causes him to focus learning effort on only those elements he personally needs to master.

2. Teaching the facts or developing the skills in ways designed to meet so far as possible each child's needs.

3. Following at once with valid, and properly motivated opportunities for each child to repeat or practice the desired reactions. The purpose is to establish the facts or the skills to the point that the correct responses will become habitual.

4. Administering a second measuring instrument which closely parallels the content of the initial or inventory instrument to determine the extent of improvement or growth.

5. Analyzing this test as a basis for discovering the class' and each individual's remaining deficiencies.

6. Remedying the defects through re-teaching and further practice.

7. Re-evaluating and if necessary, re-teaching.

Not all learning situations are as objective in content as implied above, but the test-teach-test principle surely has enough support that some adaptation or modification of the evaluative instruments and procedures suggested might be made for language expression.

The Purposes of Evaluation in Language

Evaluation of language expression is complicated by the fact that this expression is both a process and a product. Since both of these are important outcomes in a language program both must be evaluated. But before a program of evaluation can be undertaken, including the use of measurement instruments of various types, a critical analysis of the underlying skill-areas and the accurate translation of such skills, abilities, and knowledge into instructional objectives is necessary. Examination of earlier chapters in this monograph indicate the great number of complicated and interrelated objectives which may be listed. A further examination of these objectives shows, too, the number that represent intangible qualities in expression which rather successfully elude the best efforts of evaluation experts to identify and measure objectively.

Effective oral language expression depends upon the success with which a speaker chooses, arranges, and says the words which are symbols of his thoughts, and the effect they have upon his audience. In teaching children to think and to talk effectively, instructional emphasis must be placed upon the development of pleasing voice quality, clear enunciation of sounds and correct pronunciation of words, gracious manners, avoidance of common language errors, careful choice of words, thoughtful selection and arrangement of ideas, and skill in expressing ideas in sentences designed to lead the thinking of the speaker's hearers along the channels he has chosen to lead them. Equally important are the skills and attitudes which are essential to efficient and effective listening. These are the instructional objectives that must be evaluated. It is readily apparent that the skills, abilities, attitudes, and knowledge which go into the achievement of any one of them are so interwoven, and in many instances so defying of precise definition, that the evaluation task is an enormous one.

The evaluation of written expression presents a different problem. In many ways, of course, the specific skills and abilities are equally interwoven; but because of the tangible aspect of writing, many of the elements may be more adequately defined and identified. Written expression involves the mechanical factors, such as handwriting, spelling, punctuation, capitalization, form and appearance; the grammatical factors, such as usage and sentence structure; and the rhetorical factors, such as choice of words and the selection and organization of the subject matter into sentences and larger units. The mechanical and grammatical factors may be effectively evaluated. The rhetorical factors are much more intangible and are exceedingly difficult to identify and to measure objectively. Again, however, granting all the problems presented, the purpose of evaluative attempts is the determination of achievement and the identification of specific elements for instructional emphasis.

Measurement Instruments and Techniques

Instruments used to measure language achievement include (1) standardized tests, (2) scales, (3) performance tests, (4) teacher-made objective tests, (5) essay tests, and (6) miscellaneous evaluative tools such as pupil progress charts, checklists, class analysis charts, rating scales, and interviews and conferences. In addition, while not precisely an instrument, oral questioning is used extensively in measuring knowledge in the language area.[1] In general, measurement instruments and evaluative techniques used in language programs have the function of evaluating teaching and learning accomplishments. As indicated by the above listing, they are quite varied as to type, and in some instances there is considerable structural variation within the types. The selection of an evaluative or measuring instrument depends principally upon the nature of the service it is expected to perform as well as the effectiveness with which it performs this service. The instrument to use is the one that does what is expected of it in an accurate, dependable, and meaningful manner. Much of the distrust of measurement instruments has arisen through their misuse. The following principles should be observed in selecting or constructing measuring instruments or evaluative devices:

1. Clearly define the objectives of the program, or aspects of it, and select instruments or devices which provide measurement data relative to these objectives.
2. Use instruments only for purposes for which they are designed.
3. Use instruments only under conditions which are standard with respect to the product or process being evaluated.
4. Use instruments which sufficiently sample the product or process being evaluated.
5. Use instruments which provide data objectively or in which the judgment factor in arriving at data has been minimized.
6. Use caution with respect to drawing conclusions concerning the program or the performance of individuals based upon the use of a single instrument. The significance of data obtained from any evaluative instrument depends upon the validity, reliability, and suitability of the instrument as well as the way in which it was actually used.

Evaluating Specific
Language Skills and Products

Instruments and techniques for the measurement and evaluation of language expression in specific situations and of specific skills are suggested in the following sections.

---

[1] For a full discussion of evaluative instruments see, for example Harry A. Greene, A. N. Jorgensen, and J. R. Gerberich, *Measurement and Evaluation in the Elementary School* (New York: Longmans, Green & Company, 1953).

Oral expression. In spite of the social importance of oral expression, standardized evaluative instruments suitable for reliable appraisal of the skills and products are not available. Evaluation of speech and speech products, of course, may be made, but not in the same sense as in written expression in which much of the measurement may be based upon the use of standardized tests. Attempts at developing and standardizing oral scales, or clearly differentiated samples, to which a child's speech might be compared have not been successful. The difficulties involved in securing adequate sampling to be used as the bases for the scale and the cost of production and distribution are apparently overwhelming. Too, attempting to record an individual's speech seems suddenly to cause the individual not to speak normally. This is not true for all, and perhaps is becoming less true in this day of increased familiarity with recording instruments. There appears to be some possibility for the future production of standardized oral language scales as a result of the recent development of quite small transistor-powered recording devices. Presumably, recording of oral language might occur without the speaker's knowing of this. Such procedure certainly should result in recording uninhibited speech.

A scarcity of standardized instruments for measuring oral language achievement and progress does not mean that oral language cannot be evaluated. The ready availability of efficient tape recorders makes it possible for a teacher to record the speech efforts of his class. The playback of the recording allows the class, and each individual, to criticize the speech and to consider possibilities for making improvements. The speech skills and/or products on a recording made at one time of the year may be compared with those made at another time. Again, this comparison may be made a class consideration or an individual one. Use of the tape recorder may also be made by a teacher to compare children's speech products with that of a model. For example, a recording might be made of an excellent report or of a skilled interview. This might be played as the class is considering the merits of their reporting or interviewing attempts. This use is somewhat similar to the scale approach but is limited in that comparison is made with only one product. There are possibilities, however, for the further development of this idea.

In considering the evaluation of skills and abilities in oral expression the fact should not be overlooked that the appearance of the speaker and his manner of speaking plays a large part in the total expression. Recording the speech of others and comparing this with "live" speech or with another recording is an unreal comparison. Too, consideration may be given to the content of speech if this content is written. But, again, in speaking, the impact of the content is the result of the speaker's manner and his skill in producing speech sounds as well as the words themselves.

Perhaps the most practical procedure for a teacher to follow in evaluating oral expression is consistently to make use of checklists to compare expression in a particular situation with the objectives of the speech effort in that situation. The checklist on page 101 is for storytelling.

Written expression. As with oral expression pupil performances in written expression may also be appraised through the use of checklists and similar observational appraisal devices. In addition, there are many other instruments and procedures for evaluating written language skill development and achievement. These generally possess the qualities of validity, objectivity, and reliability.

The product of most written expression is a composition, whether that composition be in a story or a letter. Measurement of such composition may be done by the use of a scale, an instrument which has composition specimens arranged in order of quality from very poor to excellent. Compositions are compared with these specimens and scores assigned to them. Since a composition calls for the use of so many expressional skills, and since these are so interwoven, this kind of measurement is only a part of the total product and is necessarily subjective. These facts, and that of the limited sample as represented by a single written product, cause the evaluation of the general merit of written expression to be a major exception to the reliability, validity, and objectivity mentioned above. This does not mean that compositions may not be evaluated. It simply means that a degree of unreliability in measurement is present and that a scale has a specialized use. This unreliability may be lessened by (1) securing an extensive sampling of an individual's written expression, and (2) securing repeated ratings or evaluations of the samples by an expert judge, or (3) securing many independent evaluations by expert judges, or (4) by a combination of these three steps.

CHECKLIST FOR STORYTELLING

	Sally	Rob	Albert	Patricia	Mary	Judith	Paul
Attention of audience	✓	✓	no	✓	✓	✓	✓
Looked at audience	✓	no	no	✓	✓	no	✓
Appropriate story for audience	✓	no point	✓	✓	✓	silly	✓
Knew story well	✓	✓	no	✓	✓	no	✓
Created mood for story	✓	no	no	✓	✓	no	✓
Told story in own words	✓	✓	✓	no	✓	✓	✓
Had good beginning	✓	no	no	no	✓	no	✓
Avoided nonessentials	✓	no	no	✓	✓	✓	✓
Incorrect usages: well there	✓	✓	✓		✓		
this here	✓						
ain't	✓						
knowed	✓					✓	
Showed ease in speaking	✓	no	no	✓	✓	no	✓
Used appropriate gestures	✓						
Detracting mannerisms (identify) squirming	✓					✓	
shifting feet	✓	✓					
Voice volume adequate	✓	no	✓	✓	✓	no	✓
Pleasing voice	✓	✓	✓	✓	✓	too shrill	✓
Enunciation (which sounds)		ing					
Pronunciation (list)							
prize	✓						
interesting				✓		✓	

Little use is made of composition scales in many schools today. The better-known scales are *The Willing Scale for Measuring Written Composition* and the *Hudelson English Composition Scale*. In general, these scales call for the children to write compositions on specified topics within definite periods of time. Attention is paid in the compositions to matters of form and mechanics as well as to the content itself. The compositions may then be rated against the scales' specimens. A major factor in the profitable use of

CARL A. RUDISILL LIBRARY
LENOIR RHYNE COLLEGE

such scales is the preparation a teacher has made before judging the compositions from his class. Without following the training suggestions and engaging in an adequate amount of practice, the use of the scales will have little value. If proper preparation is made, and if a teacher will remember the subjective character of the measures yielded by the scales, these measures of the general merit of written expression can be of genuine use in a language program.

Other evaluative instruments of written expression are the objective and standardized tests which measure knowledge of grammar, usage, and skill in punctuation and capitalization. The most frequently used tests which measure these aspects of written expression are the language subtests of general achievement batteries. For example, the language subtest of the *Iowa Every-Pupil Test of Basic Skills* measures punctuation, capitalization, usage, spelling, and sentence sense. In some achievement batteries (e.g., the *Stanford Achievement Test*), the language subtest is limited to usage items. Standardized tests directed only at the measurement of language skills are also available. In some of them recognition of a language error (or of the correct form) is required. Others are more comprehensive (e.g., *Iowa Language Abilities Test*) and call for both recognition and correction of errors.

For frequent measurement of pupil progress and for measurement of learning related to a specific instructional situation, a teacher usually must develop his own evaluative materials. Teacher-made tests may consist of exercises in which pupils choose the proper item from several choices, correct incorrect expressions or forms, rewrite incorrect expressions, or fill in blanks correctly. Other instruments or procedures for evaluation which a teacher may develop include dictation exercises calling for punctuation, capitalization, sentence recognition, spelling, and usage selection. Usually a dictation exercise should deal with only one area of the mechanical skills and then only with the specific skills that are to receive, or have received, immediate instructional emphasis.

A useful procedure for evaluating written expression is the comparison of the pupils' efforts with models or with previously established standards. Such comparison may be done both by the teacher and by the individual pupil. For example, a model letter form may have been developed by the class, and individual letters may be compared with the model. A checklist may also be used in the comparison to help objectify the evaluative interpretation placed upon the comparison and as a reminder of the various items that should be compared.

Handwriting. The principal objectives of handwriting instruction are legibility and speed. Since handwriting is a highly individualistic act which requires the use of skills that involve a complex type of visual-muscular coordination, no attempt is made to achieve uniformity of style. Handwriting which appears to be normal for a child, which can be easily read by others, and which can be produced with relative ease and speed is considered acceptable. This does not mean, however, that peculiarities in the formation of letters, including peculiarities that result from improper position of the body, arm, paper, and writing instrument should not be noted and corrected. Many children have poor writing habits and these children can be aided through a differentiated program of instruction, including differentiation in evaluation, to remedy their individual difficulties. Individual evaluation of achievement and diagnosis of needs must be followed by individualized practice to remedy the deficiencies discovered.

Evaluation of handwriting occurs as a sample of writing is compared with standard writing products shown on a handwriting scale. Handwriting scales are of two types: (1) general merit scales, and (2) analytical and diagnostic scales or charts. The first is concerned with attaining a score which indicates the general merit (usually legibility) of a handwriting sample. The latter calls for the location of specific faults in the sample. The general merit scales may also be used to determine the speed with which copy has been written, although this may be done by simply counting the number of letters written during a specific lapse of time.

The scales which are used to measure handwriting quality have the disadvantage of subjectivity in the rating procedure in the same manner as do other scales. Again, too, a limited use is made of scales, particularly the merit scales, in many schools at the present time. This fact apparently is partly because of the decline in providing handwriting instruction and partly because of the feeling of many teachers that, since a copy of a particular selection must be produced for comparison with the scaled specimens, the writing is not a true sample of the child's handwriting. In addition, probably a number of teachers feel that the use of a scale brings about much uniformity in the formation of letters that is not necessary for legibility, and also possibly retards individuality. In and of themselves, however, none of these reasons appears to have enough merit to account for the general disuse. A more probable explanation is the extent to which schools do not teach specific skills and, hence, tend to regard measurement in general with distrust. Measurement points up instruction needs, usually for specific skills, a fact that is disturbing to those who take a generalized approach to instruction.

The interest today in the evaluation of handwriting centers almost entirely on such instruments as the *Freeman Chart for Diagnosing Faults in Handwriting* or the Zaner-Bloser chart *Handwriting Faults and How to Correct Them.* The latter is essentially a revision and improvement of the Freeman chart and is somewhat representative of charts published along with other parts of commercial handwriting instructional programs. The Zaner-Bloser chart provides samples of different levels of quality of the following: (1) uniformity of slant, (2) uniformity of alignment, (3) quality of line, (4) letter formation, and (5) spacing. In addition, suggestions are given as to ways to test handwriting copy for legibility, slant, spacing, alignment, size of letters, and quality of line as well as ways to correct the defects.

Diagnosis of children's handwriting faults cannot be based entirely on examination of their handwriting products. For a teacher to identify adequately and to correct poor handwriting habits, the use of scales and charts must be supplemented by observation of the children as they write. The following outline of handwriting defects and their probable causes indicates the kind of observation a teacher needs to do:[2]

Defect	*Causes*
1. Writing too slanted.	Writing arm too near body; paper tilted at greater than 30-degree angle with edge of desk; point of pen or pencil too far from fingers; writing stroke in wrong direction.

---

[2] Adapted from listings in Frank N. Freeman, *The Teaching of Handwriting* (Boston: Houghton Mifflin Co., 1915) and Gertrude Hildreth, *Learning the Three R's* (Minneapolis: Educational Publishers, Inc., 2nd ed., 1947).

2. Writing too little slanted.	Arm too far from body; fingers too near pen or pencil point; index finger alone guiding pen; paper at less than the correct angle of tilt.
3. Writing too heavy.	Pressing too heavily; pen or pencil not comfortable size.
4. Writing too light.	Pen or pencil held too obliquely or too straight; pen or pencil too large in diameter.
5. Writing too angular.	Thumb and fingers too stiff; hand and arm movement too slow; incorrect or uncomfortable body position; pen or pencil gripped too tightly.
6. Writing too irregular.	Lack of freedom of movement; lack of rhythm in movement; incorrect or uncomfortable body and arm positions and movements; pen or pencil held incorrectly.
7. Writing too widely spaced.	Attempting to write too fast; superfluous head and body movements.
8. Writing too slowly.	Irregular writing rhythm; incorrect or uncomfortable body and arm positions; too much pressure on pen or pencil; uncertainty as to letter formations; lack of adequate practice.

Emphasis in evaluating handwriting products and detecting specific errors should be upon self-evaluation by the pupils.[3] This is particularly true in the middle and upper grades after writing has been learned. Of course, at any grade level a teacher must show pupils how evaluation may be done as well as provide instruction in correcting faults. In addition to the use of standardized scales and charts the following measures may be used for evaluation:

1. Comparison of present writing with previous writing.
2. Comparison of initial sample in a lesson with final sample.
3. Keeping weekly samples for comparison.

---

[3] This is the view of the writer and many teachers and seems to conform to current educational theory; however, the majority of companies selling handwriting materials, if use of a quality or merit scale is advocated at all, suggest that the teacher make the evaluation. On the other hand, most of these companies also advocate the use of more informal measures for self-evaluation in grades three through eight.

4. Comparison with study copies in handwriting book.
5. Check sheet for listing faults.

Spelling. Evaluation in spelling should begin with an examination of the objectives of the program in the same manner as has previously been suggested for other language skills and areas. The objectives of spelling instruction as indicated in Chapter IV consists of an attitude of concern for correct spelling and the attainment of a number of habits, abilities, and skills which develop this attitude as well as the learning of the spelling of a basic core or words; therefore, an adequate evaluation program should make provision for measuring the major objectives and each related one. The principal objective—an attitude of concern about consistently spelling correctly—is a long-range goal and cannot be completely evaluated after only a year or two of spelling instruction; the same may be said for some habits and abilities. Other objectives are of shorter range and need immediate and frequent measurement. Evaluation, then, involves (1) testing how well pupils actually spell the specific words taught, (2) testing and appraisal of knowledge and use of supplemental skills and habits, and (3) observation and appraisal of habits, skills, and attitudes by teacher and pupils.

The testing of actual achievement in spelling may be approached through the use of several types of tests and testing procedures. These include:

1. Testing which is done in the regular teaching program. This includes the weekly or lesson tests and the review tests given monthly or at some other interval. It also includes semester or quarter pre-tests and final tests consisting of a sampling of the words in the spelling lessons for the period. There should be at least two or three tests given on one lesson's words, beginning with a pre-test to establish the learning goals for individual pupils.

2. Testing through the spelling section of standardized general or language achievement tests. This testing has value as a general guide to the effectiveness of a spelling program but also has definite limitations. Usually this measurement of correct spelling of a word is determined by the pupil's selection of the correct form from among several incorrect spellings. What is measured is probably something different from the recall ability needed when writing. Such tests also may be more directly related to reading ability or vocabulary development of a child than to his ability to spell specific words.

3. Comparison of testing results with a standardized spelling scale. A

teacher may compare the spelling ability of the pupils in his class on specific words with the data given in a scale such as *The New Iowa Spelling Scale.*

Test procedure. Research evidence indicates that the most efficient and economical way to test ability to spell specific words is by teacher dictation of the list of words. Words are dictated in the following manner, in which the pupil writes only the word— not the sentence:

boat	The *boat* came near the shore.	*boat*
days	There are seven *days* in the week.	*days*

Of major importance is the procedure followed in the correction of spelling tests: each pupil should correct his own test. This technique, which is called the "corrected test," has been called by Horn "the most fruitful single learning activity per unit of time that has yet been devised."[4]

Observational procedure. Those aspects of the spelling program that include the habitual use of the dictionary, proofreading of written work, and the accurate hearing of words as well as attitudes toward spelling cannot adequately be evaluated by the use of tests. True, knowledge of dictionary parts and the skills needed for their use, knowledge of steps in proofreading, and skill in the application of phonetic and structural principles may be tested in objective fashion, but our interest is primarily in the day-to-day application of these things which aid children in spelling correctly and being concerned about their spelling. The teacher may best appraise the development of attitudes and habits by the use of charts or checklists for the recording of observations made at periodic intervals or somewhat continuously.

Pupil self-evaluation. As in other areas of learning pupils should actively take part in evaluation whenever possible. The following are some ways in which pupils may participate:[5]

1. Keeping a progress chart of weekly scores made on spelling tests.
2. Keeping a progress chart on written activities containing mis-

---

[4] Ernest Horn, *Teaching Spelling: What Research Says to the Teacher* (Washington, D.C.: National Education Association, 1954), p. 18.

[5] Walter T. Petty, *Improving Your Spelling Program* (San Francisco: Chandler Publishing Company, 1959), pp. 62–63.

spellings. For example: How many words per 50 or 100 words written were misspelled? Record this number and periodically make a similar check.

3. Keeping a record of the proofreading of written work.

4. Correcting individual spelling tests, recording the scores, and analyzing the errors made.

5. Keeping individual spelling lists of words needed in writing.

6. Comparing handwriting specimens periodically to determine the progress in writing.

7. Using the tape recorder to determine improvement in pronunciation.

8. Keeping a record of words looked up in the dictionary—or some other record of actual dictionary use.

9. Analyzing the procedure used in learning to spell a word to determine if all steps are being followed.

10. Helping others in the class with their spelling in order to keep up class morale.

Bibliography

LANGUAGE ARTS CURRICULUM AND METHODS

Commission on the English Curriculum, National Council of Teachers of English, *Language Arts for Today's Children.* New York: Appleton-Century-Crofts, Inc., 1954.

Dawson, Mildred A. and Marian Zollinger, *Guiding Language Learning.* Yonkers-on-Hudson: World Book Company, 1957.

Greene, Harry A. and Walter T. Petty, *Developing Language Skills in the Elementary School.* Boston: Allyn and Bacon, Inc., 1959.

Herrick, Virgil E. and Leland B. Jacobs, eds., *Children and the Language Arts.* Englewood Cliffs, N.J.: Prentice-Hall, Inc., 1955.

Strickland, Ruth G., *The Language Arts in the Elementary School.* Boston: D. C. Heath and Company, 2nd ed., 1957.

Teaching Language in the Elementary School, Forty-third Yearbook of the National Society for the Study of Education, Part II. Chicago: University of Chicago Press, 1944.

Tidyman, Willard F. and Marguerite Butterfield, *Teaching the Language Arts.* New York: McGraw-Hill Book Company, 2nd ed., 1960.

HANDWRITING

Freeman, Frank N., *What Research Says to the Teacher: Teaching Handwriting.* Washington, D.C.: Department of Classroom Teachers and American Educational Research Association of the National Education Association, 1954.

The Handwriting Committee, *Handwriting Today.* Cambridge, Mass.: New England School Development Council, September, 1954.

Herrick, Virgil E., *Comparison of Practices in Handwriting Advocated by Nineteen Commercial Systems of Handwriting Instruction.* Madison, Wisc.: Committee on Research in Basic Skills, University of Wisconsin, July, 1960.

GRAMMAR AND USAGE

Marckwardt, Albert H. and Fred G. Walcott, *Facts about Current English Usage.* New York: Appleton-Century-Crofts, Inc., 1938.

Pooley, Robert C., *Teaching English Usage.* New York: Appleton-Century-Crofts, Inc., 1946.

————, *Teaching English Grammar.* New York: Appleton-Century-Crofts, Inc., 1957.

LISTENING

Anderson, V. A., *Improving the Child's Speech*. New York: Oxford University Press, Inc., 1953.

Nichols, R. G. and T. R. Lewis, *Listening and Speaking*. Dubuque, Iowa: Wm. C. Brown Co., 1954.

Pratt, Edward and Harry A. Greene, *Training Children to Listen*, A Monograph for Elementary Teachers, No. 80. Evanston, Ill.: Row, Peterson and Company, 1955.

Russell, David H. and Elizabeth F. Russell, *Listening Aids Through the Grades*. New York: Bureau of Publications, Teachers College, Columbia University, 1959.

Whyte, William H., Jr., *Is Anybody Listening?* New York: Simon and Schuster, Inc., 1952.

SPEECH

Ogilvie, Mardel, *Speech in the Elementary School*. New York: McGraw-Hill Book Company, Inc., 1954.

Rasmussen, Carrie, *Speech Methods in the Elementary School*. New York: The Ronald Press Company, 1947.

Van Riper, Charles and Katharine G. Butler, *Speech in the Elementary Classroom*. New York: Harper & Brothers, 1955.

SPELLING

Fitzgerald, James A., *A Basic Life Spelling Vocabulary*. Milwaukee: The Bruce Publishing Company, 1951.

———, *The Teaching of Spelling*. Milwaukee: The Bruce Publishing Company, 1951.

Greene, Harry A., *The New Iowa Spelling Scale*. Iowa City: Bureau of Educational Research and Service, State University of Iowa, 1955.

Hildreth, Gertrude, *Spelling in the Modern School Program*. New York: Holt, Rinehart & Winston, Inc., 1955.

Horn, Ernest, *What Research Says to the Teacher: Teaching Spelling*. Washington, D.C.: Department of Classroom Teachers and American Educational Research Association of the National Education Association, 1954.

Petty, Walter T., *Improving Your Spelling Program*. San Francisco: Chandler Publishing Company, 1959.

———, and Gus, P. Plessas, "Challenging Superior Spellers," *Elementary School Journal*, LIX (December, 1958), pp. 154–57.

WRITING

Applegate, Mauree, *Helping Children Write*. Evanston: Row, Peterson and Company, 1954.

Association for Childhood Education International, *When Children Write.* Washington, D.C.: The Association, 1955.

Burrows, Alvina T., *What Research Says to the Teacher: Teaching Composition.* Washington, D.C.: Department of Classroom Teachers and American Educational Research Association of the National Education Association, n.d.

————, *et al., They All Want to Write.* Englewood Cliffs, N.J.: Prentice-Hall, Inc., 1952.

Index